STANLEY SPENCER

STANLEY SPENCER

by his brother Gilbert

illustrated by the author

REDCLIFFE
Bristol

First published in 1961
by Victor Gollancz Ltd
Reissued by Redcliffe Press Ltd
49 Park Street, Bristol in 1991

ISBN 1 872971 16 4

Printed and bound by
The Longdunn Press Ltd, Bristol

To

Margaret Ursula Spencer

1898–1959

And To

Glyn And Tudor

"Art is 90 per cent living."

—*Stan to Gil*, 1952

FOREWORD

My brother Stanley was born at "Fernley", Cookham, on June 30th, 1891, one year, one month, and four days before I was. We remained together until, with my kit-bag over my shoulder, I walked out of the Beaufort Hospital at Bristol on my way to Aldershot in November 1915. As I walked down the drive then, I could see him, carrying bucket and brooms, on his way to the Hospital Chapel, an interesting assignment when you consider what was to follow.

This account of our boyhood together, and of our family, and of Stanley's development as a painter, should be regarded as a kind of backcloth. I am not writing the life of Sir Stanley Spencer; that would be beyond me. But we followed the same profession. In my early days I even attempted some religious paintings, but soon abandoned that, realising that I could get along better in other ways; though not before my brother had observed, after seeing my painting of the Crucifixion, in which I had used Father as a model, "I don't know what it is, but when Gil paints Pa his pictures seem to be all right".

And so I prefer to write about "Stan". In our profession a backcloth is generally used to set off a portrait. It is chosen with great care: attention is given to colour, pattern and design, and finally the light is so arranged as to sharpen the features and characteristics of the model. My backcloth has also been carefully chosen.

CHAPTER I

COOKHAM AT THE turn of the century was, like many Thames-side villages, strongly imbued with a spirit of independence, of a kind which is more usually associated with islands. Surrounded as it was at times by floods that cut the village off from the outside world, its isolation, which for us was so attractive, was seldom disturbed; only when the regular summer visitors arrived to take up their rooms in the beflowered hotels and cottages.

True, the railway had been there for some years but, unlike the motor-car later, it had not much altered Cookham's way of life. Folk sitting in their cottages could still call out "Good night!" to Sammy Sandalls or to Mr. Plumbridge with nothing more by which to recognise the passerby than the sound of his feet on the ground. This method of identification was not as difficult as it might seem, for the change in the tone of, say, Sammy Sandalls' footsteps as he turned into the alley by the Nest was most marked.

And so, except for festive occasions and the visitations of the "beanfeasters", Cookham was a quiet village, so much so that at times the sound of the water passing through the weir could almost be heard in the village.

My father was reticent about our ancestry; he was not really very interested in it. All that he did bother to record was written on the flyleaf of what might be regarded as the family Bible. Here he noted that he, William Spencer, was born on September 16th, 1845, and that Anna Caroline Spencer (née Slack) was born on September 15th, 1851. Then followed the names of his children: William, George and Annie with the month, date and year against their names; Harold and Florence with the month and date only; the dates, months and years in which Percy Julius, Horace,

Sydney, Stanley and I were born are not recorded. Bracketed together are Gertrude and Ernest, who died in infancy. Finally it was recorded that W. G. Spencer (my eldest brother) married Johanna Simon of Bonn, Germany, and that Harold Spencer married Natalie Balloo of Gibraltar. There is no doubt that all this was written at one and the same time and late in his life.

There were occasions when we were given glimpses of distant times, but generally Father's characteristic reply to our enquiries was that we were descended from robbers and thieves, or that we had come to this country in the reign of Edward II.

There are other possibilities. Although I do not remember any reference at home to any other Spencers, "Spencers" was and still is a place name in the district, which suggests that even if we ourselves were not direct descendants, at some time in the past there had been other Spencers at Cookham or in the district who had belonged to the aristocracy or the landed gentry.

And there were times when Father adopted a less caustic attitude towards our enquiries, and if what he was able to tell us then was still limited; it at least had more of the stamp of authenticity about it. When he was in one of these more communicative moods we were able to learn that he was the eldest of three children (the other two being Julius and Lizzie) by the second wife of Julius Spencer, who hailed from Wooburn in Bucks and who settled at Vine Cottage, Cookham, where he set up as a master builder, probably a little before 1830. It is not easy today, with the building trade so highly organised, to appreciate what this status meant a hundred or more years ago; but every village of any size—and Cookham gave its name to the Rural District Council—had its master builder then, and had to have one.

My grandfather had died before our time, and his business had ceased to exist; but first my step-uncle, John, had succeeded to it, and had retired in rather unusual circumstances. A hot-tempered and heavily bewhiskered man, he returned home one day, threw down his bag, and announced to his assembled family that as he had supported them for half his life, it was now their turn to support him. And for the rest of his life he devoted himself to his much-loved fishing, which he carried on from the old tarred wooden bridge over the Fleet on the moor. From this point his rods, bent almost double from experience and disappointment, looked down on the sly old pike who knew Uncle John as well as he knew them.

As children we could just remember the old builder's yard at the back of Vine Cottage. There was sand still lying around, with which we used to play. Tiles were stacked against the side of a tottering building, and beneath the eaves of its roof were slung one or two old ladders. My Uncle John and Aunt Catherine continued to live there.

It was difficult for us to imagine then that it could ever have been a flourishing business. My father's recollection of having helped to cut the pegs for the tiles for "Church Gate" gives something of a clue. Other buildings of his, such as the semi-detached villas of Fernley and Belmont, built for Father and Uncle Julius to occupy on their marriages, and the schools, still stand as monuments to his integrity as a builder. As architecture, however, they have to be confessed to rather than boasted about. They must have looked painfully out of place amidst the old cottages of the Cookham of those days. For one thing, fun and games with cast iron was by then very much in vogue, and my grandfather made generous use of this material in the external presentation of Fernley and Belmont. And to make matters worse, it was always said that the cottages in Fred Walker's picture called "Geese in Cookham Village" were pulled down to make way for us.

It is quite possible that Mr. Wiggs' building establishment, which flourished in my childhood, was the successor to my grandfather's business, and in describing it I may be giving a fairly accurate account of the Vine Cottage establishment of Grandpa Spencer. It was at the top of the village, on the fringe of the moor, and followed very much the pattern of Vine Cottage. There was the same kind of long wooden building in which all the indoor work was carried on, though this one had two storeys; in the lower the yard tools and so forth were stored, and in the upper, reached by outside steps, the carpentry and joinery were done—though it must be said that this work spread round the side and the back of the house. The shafts of sunlight through the window fell on to a long carpenter's bench which appeared to be floating on a sea of nice clean shavings. Among these shavings the carpenters moved about on their respective tasks, with large flat pencils behind their ears and their apron pockets bulging with tools. There was a generous amplitude about all this. Time seemed unlimited. The staff, about six in number, would have been regular employees, all Cookhamites, and probably none had ever worked for anyone else. Occasionally there would be an addition to their number: when a coffin was needed, it could be seen perched on a couple of trestles at one end of the room, and Mrs. Wigg would be busily engaged lining it—lovingly, as my mother used to say.

Everything was brought by horse and cart to the site where a building was being erected. Building was then a matter of ladders up which men carried hods of bricks on their shoulders, and scaffolding skilfully roped together and resting secure in large barrels of earth. The work could at times be dangerous, and it is small wonder that on one occasion Eliza Sandalls, pointing in the direction of the malt houses where Sammy Sandalls could be seen mending one of the cowls, commented: "Father has no business to be up there at his time of life."

My father's unpredictable information about his ancestors—which once included the claim, not to be taken seriously, that his grandmother was a washerwoman—did not include any explanation of why Grandpa Spencer elected to become a builder. Nor did he throw any light on his love of music. Grandfather did not play any instrument, as far as I know, but what he did do was to build up a village choir which he himself conducted, and by all accounts a very good choir. In those days a choir still

GRANDPA SPENCER'S CHOIR CROSSING TO CLIVEDEN

retained some of the traditions of the itinerant musicians: it would be summoned here and there, more often to sing at important houses in the district than perhaps anything else. The concert hall had not as yet interposed itself between them and their old patrons.

The choir was much in demand in many parts of the Home Counties. Their method of travelling would usually have been by horse wagons, or perhaps by Brunel's railway. But one not infrequent journey they did on foot, and this one proved of significance to us later. Cliveden House, which could be seen from the village, high up in Cliveden Woods, was then occupied by the Duke of Westminster, and the choir was, from time to time, summoned to perform at his house-parties.

One can imagine the singers collecting outside Vine Cottage, waiting for Grandpa Spencer to join them. There would be a fair sprinkling of Slacks and Spencers among them. Moving off, they would follow what was to become one of our favourite walks, and later was of considerable importance to Stan. It all still exists—Ship Lane, Mill Lane, and the path down to My Lady Ferry. Here they crossed the river, and afterwards would climb up through the woods to the house. Singing as they climbed, their voices from among the trees could be heard across the river. No wonder we got it firmly into our heads that Handel wrote his Water Music for one of these occasions. And we imbibed almost with our mother's milk the knowledge that "Rule Britannia" was first sung at Cliveden House.

This romantic account of the visits to Cliveden, as it was colourfully told to us, made a deep and lasting impression. And if the third of my grandfather's interests is in sharp contrast to these lovely occasions, the fact that in the pursuit of it he was from time to time brought to his knees in supplication to Almighty God discloses a humility which he retained throughout his lifetime.

As young children, Stan and I, in pursuit of our common interest of trying to find something to play with, would occasionally resort to the cupboard beneath the stairs. This cupboard was as black as night and smelled very musty. We would fumble in the darkness for anything we could lay our hands on: odd brooms; a piano trolley; objects that in the darkness remained shapeless to our peering eyes. One object which we managed to unearth was particularly surprising. I think Stan found it first; he was more inquisitive than I was, and my recollection is that he held it up to show to me. We played with it for a while and when we grew weary of playing, we put everything back in the cupboard in accordance with my mother's instructions, and shut the door. What we had, in fact, found was an honest-to-God pair of good Victorian handcuffs—to which, later, was added a truncheon. In view of my father's references to our criminal ancestry, it might seem that we had unearthed a

WE FIND THE HANDCUFFS IN THE CUPBOARD

family skeleton. But the truth is that Grandpa had at one time been the constable of the village; and we were told that he never went out to apprehend anyone without first going down on his knees.

About Grandpa Spencer's first wife very little is known. It is possible that he married her before coming to Cookham. She produced a family—of whom Uncle John was the second son—which I believe ventured out into the world with success. Having done so, she disappeared from the scene altogether.

After her death my grandfather married again, his bride this time being a woman named Gosling. She had come to Cookham to take up a post as governess at one of the big houses, and she hailed from Seaton in Devonshire.

After his death she moved from Vine Cottage to the Nest, a cottage next door to us, which in my childhood was entirely submerged by ivy. She too died before our time, but we heard occasional references to her. That "God's Eye" (the framed representation of the Almighty's eye which hung on the wall, an ever-present reminder that God sees all) was moved from Vine Cottage to the Nest when she moved is perhaps a sufficient indication that she shared Grandpa Spencer's severe and probably puritanical views. It rather looks also as though she too had some responsibility for our entry into the musical world, by responding to my father's persistent entreaties when it had been decided that it was my Uncle Julius who was going to be taught by Dr. Thorn, the organist. It has been said that the final decision was arrived at by the tossing of a coin. Probably she was a disciplinarian: Father's story that as a boy he had to walk to Marlow each week to get the yeast for bread-making showed that she ruled her family, as does the account of her issuing from the Nest each morning carrying a clothes prop, with which she tapped on Father's bedroom window to rouse him.

From the Nest she often popped into Fernley, where she passed the time sitting by the window in the drawing-room, watching the passers-by and the life of the village in general.

One day, while she was so engaged, the Duke of Westminster called to see Father. Like many another duke he was careless of his appearance. As soon as he had gone, she called to Father: "William, who was that man?" and having been told, with much "hushing", exclaimed: "Poor man, poor man."

What they all looked like I can only judge now by memories of a heavy photograph album with a brass clasp that used to be in our drawing-room. Here were photographs not only of our grandparents but of innumerable other relations as well. Many of these photographs were faded: to see them you had to tilt the album. But by tilting them this way and that, eventually the images of my grandparents would emerge and by the same process so did the features of a lot of other relations. To me the photographs all looked very much the same. These people seemed dignified, severe, God-fearing, and goodness knows what besides; perhaps hard and cruel. Not one of them wore a kindly smile. But as all their heads, we were told, were gripped in a vice, that was perhaps understandable. One of them, we understood, had been guilty of some kind of fiddle. When we met him on our walks, we always spoke to him, in accordance with my father's dictum that "you should never point the finger of scorn at a man once he had purged his offence"; but one of the matters on which, as a family, we were all agreed was that Uncle Tom looked shifty—to which my father would add, with finality, "Eyes too close".

The womenfolk were all curls, bosoms, bustles and crinolines, and in such numbers; the album was so packed with relations that it was almost impossible to close it—Spencers, Slacks, Poultons, Hatches, Jordans and Llewellyns, all swelling the number of those who lived in and around Cookham.

On my mother's side, Wooburn appears to have had its attractions also. Her mother, whose name I believe was Mary, was the daughter of a Mr. and Mrs. Barnett who lived there. Wooburn at that time would have been more industrialised than Cookham. Glory Mills, Soho Mills and

Jackson's Mills had been established long before my childhood, and possibly the Barnetts had some connection with one or other of them. It was often asserted, and sometimes vigorously, that Grandma (to us, Great Grandma) Barnett was a Jewess, though some denied this.

About this time the village of Cookham was passing through a crisis, of a kind which must have borne some resemblance to others before it, not only there but in the country generally. There was much poverty and hardship, aggravated in this Thames-side village by severe flooding. The Industrial Revolution was closing in, and reached Cookham in tangible form when Mr. Burrows set up his shoe factory at Lullabrook Manor. He devised a scheme by which many of the little parlours in the cottages were given over to cobbling, with shoe lathes installed. It can be assumed that some increase in prosperity resulted.

It was to this business, as overseer and chief cutter, that John Slack, an Irishman, was appointed. How he came by the job, whether he came direct from Ireland, where he lived in Cookham, how he met Miss Barnett of Wooburn—nothing is known of all this. But the upshot of it was that he married my grandmother, and they too settled somewhere in the village.

For a time, it seems, all went well. One envisages him visiting the various cottages, examining, advising and encouraging. The shoes when completed were taken to Lullabrook, where they were packed and despatched "all over the world"—"Burrows shoes went all over the world" we were told.

But Burrows' homespun notion of industrialisation proved no answer to what was happening in other parts of the country. In due course the hurry and scurry of mechanisation began to make itself felt at Cookham. Grandpa Slack was only partially able to extricate himself from it.

Just as there was nothing to explain why Julius Spencer decided to set up as a builder, neither do we know why, to meet this personal crisis, Grandma Slack either started or took over a grocer's business in the village—the business known to us as Stuchberrys Stores (P. & S. Thompson Ltd.). But this is what she did, and I believe that it was here that my mother (the youngest of a fair-sized family) was born in 1851. Between Grandpa's dwindling work at the factory and hers at the shop, they seem to have eked out a livelihood, and the fact that ultimately he was able to retire to a red-brick house, called Cliveden View, which he built at Cookham Rise, suggests that there were savings as well.

Village grocers' shops are perhaps less affected by change than most things, and although the business was expanding when I knew it, in many ways it must still have been as it was when my mother was a child. There was a fairly even flow of customers during the week, encouraged no doubt by the fact that although it was primarily a grocer's, it also stocked a fairly extensive assortment of other things—pots and pans, kettles, brooms and brushes, and a variety of earthenware. Paraffin oil had a kind of nuisance value; no one wanted to mess around with paraffin and then have to weigh out butter and lard. As children we were always being sent for a gallon of oil, and Mr. Plum, who managed the shop for Stuchberrys, was always irritated and never wanted to go and fetch it.

But on Fridays the whole atmosphere of the shop changed. Practically the whole of the floor space in front of the counter, except for a narrow alleyway up to the counter, became covered with baskets which during the day were gradually filled up with the weekly orders, finally to be despatched to the big houses and the cottages, and across field paths, meadows and marshes to outlying farms, on the back of a boy who strained ever forward towards his objective—and who received a shilling for his day's work.

The children seem to have been very much around, and it is more than likely that they took a hand in helping their mother in the shop. My mother, to have become such an observant little girl, must have put in a good deal of time perched on some vantage point. The customers can scarcely have been aware that all their little foibles, all their likes and dislikes, were being so closely noted and their voices so skilfully imitated. But that was what little Anna Caroline was up to. We know how well she did it because she sometimes gave us her precise recollections and imitations, and very good little portraits of village personalities they were.

It is difficult to imagine how she contrived to practise and develop her skill in this art against the austere background of her home, but that she must have succeeded is made apparent by the accounts she used to give us of visiting many cottages in the village and delighting them with her performances. One almost sees her, still in the pinafore stage, popping in and out of the houses, scoring successes all round. But these performances could only have been before carefully selected audiences, who must not be allowed to discover that they in turn were probably being portrayed elsewhere.

She was rewarded for these entertainments with cake and elderberry wine. On one occasion, after a particularly successful production, she returned to the shop in a tipsy condition. Forthwith she was banished to her room, where she had to remain on a very meagre diet but eked out with some appetising dishes which were brought up the lean-to roof to her by their old servant.

When she returned to family life again, her brother John was waiting for her with an open Bible and the paraphernalia required for the signing of the pledge spread out in front of him. What a scene this was: the black-coated and, one might fairly say, overbearing man and the little girl whose only crime had really not been so heinous.

The pews at Cookham Church at that time had high backs, so Mother told us. This would imply that they had high fronts as well, since one pew's back would be another pew's front. They were entered by doors, and to all intents and purposes were like little rooms with no ceilings. The grown-ups alone could see over the tops, and then only when they stood up. The little ones must have had a very dull time of it.

I too can remember as a child the anguishing experience of the very long and often tedious sermons and the Litany

Sundays. But by then the high-back pews had been replaced. Maybe this was done to prevent any repetition of an occurrence that Mother related to us.

The Slack children usually went to church with their parents, but sometimes the old servant took them instead. And on one occasion she apparently decided to enliven the visit in her own way. It was the custom, in those days of high-backed pews, for the verger sometimes to sally forth from his pew during the sermon, proceed down the aisle, and here and there open a pew door and take a peep inside. The preacher may have felt complimented on this occasion by the silent attention of the Slacks, hidden away in their pew, but on the other hand it may have been this very silence which aroused the suspicions of the verger and prompted him to open their door and look in. My mother's description of what he saw was attractive. It included sandwiches and cakes, and she even went so far as to suggest that a table cloth had been spread out over the seat.

Another vivid recollection of hers was of the day when, at a Sunday school treat at Burnham Beeches, a horse ran away with her and she was carried along, upside down, with all her petticoats and drawers (unmentionables, as she always referred to these garments) in full display, with the horse spurred on to further effort by the helpless shouts of the crowd, who gave her up for dead.

But like Father, she did not talk a lot to us about these early times. It can be assumed, though, that she went to the dame school at the top of the village. She certainly had very clear and beautiful handwriting; and to a certain extent—more so than any other member of the family—Stan inherited this.

The photograph album in the drawing-room was not wholly given up to relations; now and then something different managed to squeeze itself in. One photograph which I have in mind was of a later date than most of the others. It was taken in our own lifetime. In spite of this, however, it was fading very badly, and no amount of tilting made any difference. But it was possible to perceive that it was of a rather odd-looking procession, and we were told that the occasion was the Diamond Jubilee, as celebrated in Cookham.

We had been told much about the Diamond Jubilee of Queen Victoria, and the descriptions of it were dazzling in the extreme. But the Jubilee that was described to us was not Cookham's Jubilee. It was a world event, an astonishing spectacle with its mile-long procession, and not just one band, but band after band; and elephants with rajahs on their backs; and camels; and natives from Darkest Africa—seemingly all the peoples of the earth taking part, most of them British subjects and the others well in the running for election.

In London, then, all the pomp and glory of Victoria's Empire parading along its beflagged streets. And in Cookham? Alas, no rajahs on the backs of elephants there. In point of fact, there never was a more disorganised and bedraggled-looking affair than the Diamond Jubilee procession at Cookham. From the fading silhouette of the village, flags in disarray could be dimly picked out, strung across the street, tied to water-spouts or through windows to bedsteads. These flags looked as though they had been out before and in all weathers; many of them had probably done their stint for the Crimea, and some of them might even have been unfurled for Waterloo.

And what a procession! Higgledy-piggledy, this way and that, dresses dragging in the dust, no left-righting, no martial spirit, no bands—just a straggle along the village street of a thoroughly untidy and undisciplined-looking crowd. And these were the people whose way of life had made them masters all over the world!

Yet there was usually a professionalism about the Victorians, a kind of super-expertise. Amateurism they would have regarded as the tail wagging the dog. Certainly Father would not have countenanced the idea of amateur soldiering. The Army was a job and a career. How he would have been startled by the thought of a conscript army of five million. To have been conscripted for the Crimea! Why,

STAN AND I LEAD THE PROCESSION AT THE DIAMOND JUBILEE

it that had been possible, Father and Uncle Julius might have taken part in the Charge of the Light Brigade!

Father's contribution to the procession was, none the less, to place himself at the head of it. As he appears on the photograph, he is turning and looking back at the advancing villagers. He is wearing the usual black frock coat, and one is just able to observe the fringes of a fierce black moustache and beard. But he had not placed himself at the head for reasons of vanity, nor was he so much concerned with the disarray of the procession behind him as he was with two little figures leading it.

They are dressed in white frocks and coats, and wear hats that anticipate the frilled lampshades which came into fashion shortly afterwards. Built up on wire frames, frills upon frills, they were of extreme discomfort, and Stan and I much preferred the red tam-o-shanters which we wore on less important occasions.

Father's reason for placing us at the head of the procession was a practical one. He felt that had we been put at the back we would have lagged behind, and that if we were placed in the front we would not be overtaken. And we weren't overtaken. We probably joined the procession as it was forming outside the church after the thanksgiving service, to perambulate through the village to the moor for the festivities. Teas for the very old—and there may have been one or two who remembered Waterloo; teas for the young—and there would have been many like Stan and me who could remember nothing. There were three-legged races, and there was the inevitable egg and spoon race, the eggs being dummies lent by Mr. Hatch. There may have been some grinning through horse collars, and saucings with treacle and bags of flour: I say there may have been, as we had heard of this, in an atmosphere of disapproval, as a relic of barbarism.

With a tug-of-war and the National Anthem the proceedings ended and the children returned home, each carrying a rather misshapen Union Jack and a Jubilee Mug. our mugs were in the kitchen cupboard when I left home in 1920: they had been there ever since 1897.

CHAPTER II

As I have said, change came slowly to Cookham. The period between the Crimea and the Boer War was one of tranquillity. The industrial revolution, though it had touched the village, had not engulfed it. Even the railway had brought few changes.

But one very important change, as far as we were concerned, the railway did effect. It enabled Miss Gosling to travel from Seaton to Cookham. In earlier days the village had been isolated to a degree; and in consequence, one imagines, there must have been much intermarrying. Traditionally, courtships and romances had their beginnings in the village school. We ourselves were said to have over seventy relatives in and around the village. So that when Grandpa Spencer chose someone from distant Devon as his bride, it must have been something in the nature of a matrimonial revolution for Cookham.

Our parents, on the other hand, reverted to the traditional old-fashioned romance of the days before the railway. They had been pupils together at the dame school at the top of the village, and their common interest in music brought them together in Grandpa Spencer's choir. "Birdie" Slack's voice (and she was nicknamed "Birdie" on account of her singing) would have been one of those that could be heard among the trees in the romantic setting of Cliveden Woods.

The date of their marriage is implied in the inscription on the flyleaf of the family Bible: "Given by Mr. Cusack to William Spencer with best wishes for his welfare, June 26, 1873. Let the word of Christ dwell in you richly in all wisdom. Colossians 3–16." We always regarded this as their wedding day.

After their marriage they settled in at Fernley, and shortly afterwards my uncle Julius, having married a Miss Jenny Lloyd from Scotland, moved into Belmont, next door. And there our parents and our uncle and aunt remained for the rest of their lives.

These semi-detached villas, before they had been mercifully hidden behind virginia creeper, were very ugly, with their yellow bricks, cast-iron railings and slate tiles. And yet we grew to love them like no other place on earth.

There must have been some financial arrangement between Grandpa Spencer and his two sons. What it was would not, of course, have been our concern, but I know that Father paid rent to "Uncle Jew" for the whole of the sixty-odd years he lived there.

In his youth Father had been organist at Cookham Church, and how he came to be translated from there to St. Jude's, Whitechapel, must be a matter for speculation or research. The only musical connection we ever heard of was Dr. Thorn, his organ master.

Through his connection with St. Jude's we became familiar with the names of Canon Barnett and of Toynbee Hall—without knowing much about it, or about Mrs. Barnett, with whom Father quarrelled fiercely over the choir practices. At a dinner in London at which Father was present, one of the topics discussed was whether it was wicked to go on the river on Sundays. Canon Barnett called across to him, "What do they do down at Cookham, Spencer?" to which Father answered, "The publicans and sinners go on the river and the Pharisees sit on the bank and watch them."

He was then prosperous. His pupils came from influential families, and among them were the children of Mr. Justice Vaughan Williams. His pupils kept him in London for most of the week, and it was often cited to us later as proof of his great love of Cookham that he was prepared to give up much of his London work, including St. Jude's, so that he could be at home more.

Later he was appointed organist and choir master at

Hedsor Church and, while retaining some of his London connections, he soon began to get pupils in and around Cookham. Many of them were widely dispersed around the district but he reached them all on his lady's bicycle, which was his only means of transport throughout the whole of his professional life. Out in all weathers, with his music case slung over the handle-bars, he was a familiar figure. His exit line after breakfast, "I hope to be home at half-past nine," lost none of its sting by being so often repeated.

A nicely engraved brass plate on the gate, besides stating that he was the organist of St. Nicholas, Hedsor, set out his other qualifications as well.

FATHER ON HIS ROUNDS

Life at home in those, for us, far-off days sounded very grand. There was much ordering of Parsons from the King's Arms stables—a very smart and up-stagey thing to do. There were grand concerts in London—evening dress, boiled shirts and toppers (things we very rarely saw in our days)—servants and a nurse—all the trappings of position. "We heard some music by a new composer named Sibelius —I rather liked it," Father wrote about this time.

But although we were led to believe that Father had given up his London connections on account of his love of Cookham, another reason may have been that his growing family, advancing towards school age, would soon be brought within the scope of the 1870 Education Act. To many the Act was regarded as a great advance; but if Father thought so too, at the same time it presented him with problems.

The idea of her children going to the National School did not appeal to Mother, and other parents in the village felt the same way. Why Father did not meet Mother's feelings about the National School (later, Stan and I were threatened with it) by sending Will and Harold to Maidenhead, as he did later with Florence, Percy and Horace, is not clear. There could have been no money difficulties then, such as arose later.

Anyway, he decided to counter the Education Act by starting a school of his own. He was a self-educated man. I think he went after his education through the company he sought, and in this way he achieved a wide range of knowledge. Greek, Latin and French claimed his interest. He was widely read. I think he had taken more than a peep at Euclid. He adored astronomy. I have a feeling he knew some tricks in chemistry. Grammar, geography and arithmetic he knew enough of, and poetry by the bucketful. With the organ, piano, rudiments of harmony and singing, as stated on the brass plate on our front gate, what more could a village ask in an expanding world if their sons and daughters were to avoid the Education Act of 1870?

A photograph has survived, a less faded one than many,

in which Father is to be seen at the bottom of our garden beneath the walnut tree surrounded by his pupils, four at least of whom are his own children. One or two have climbed into the tree. But there is no sign of the school! Whether Sammy Sandalls, next door, got any rent, or whether his rent was reduced by Uncle Julius, who now owned his and a number of the other houses, or whether indeed he was even asked, the fact was that our school building was in his garden; and except for us, who entered it through a gate in the wall, the pupils reached it through his garden.

The building was a very simple structure, corrugated iron throughout, lined inside with matchboarding, stained a kind of iodine colour, and with a stove, in front of which was a basin of steaming water to prevent us from suffocating. As for the pupils, their attendance may have solved for them the social problem of how to avoid the National School, but their appearance in the photograph suggests that some of them could not have been making much of a financial contribution. Of course, fashions in those days were different; but with some of those pupils, it was not so much a case of fashion—it was more as though they had grown into what others had grown out of.

It is difficult to see how Father would have managed to keep both the school and the round of music pupils going at the same time. He would have strongly disapproved of neglecting any of them, and it may have been for this reason that he decided to give up the school and devote his whole time to his music pupils again. These were to include Lady Desborough, Lord Boston, and Rosamund and Beatrix Lehmann. Rosamund has told me he used to recite poems which he had written to her while she was supposed to be learning to sing. He liked this kind of life better than the school under the walnut tree; it gave him the chance to think about his poems as he rode about the countryside.

Perhaps the photograph may have been a farewell gesture, for long before our day he had transferred the school to the two Miss Georges—nieces of Mr. Sutton near-by. He probably did this after he had piloted Will,

Annie and Harold through their schooling. For the rest of his life he devoted himself to teaching music and to the organ at Hedsor.

The stories of my brother Willie's feats as a child prodigy made a deep impression on us as soon as we were old enough to appreciate them. We heard of him as a child in velveteen, who, before he could reach the pedals, was playing at the Duke of Westminster's before exalted personages including Edward Prince of Wales. He could play preludes and fugues from memory.

In a *Times* review of one of the concerts given by students of the Royal College of Music under Stanford, he was mentioned before Clara Butt, and often afterwards declared that he had "heralded Clara Butt".

He gave "grand" evening concerts at Maidenhead, for which Parsons was ordered, and the family went off in style to hear him and, as often as not, Harold as well, who shared the programmes with him. It was the rule in those days to call such concerts "grand", and I can well remember the notices, pasted on boards and placed centrally on the railing in front of the house. They were set out with great care and dignity, down to the time for ordering carriages.

Will was amused to read in the local press, after one of these concerts, that Mr. Willie Spencer was "in his usual good form at the piano". But he was not so amused on another occasion when, during a concert, the singer whom he was accompanying, a powerfully built bass, reached a line in his song which ran "And I slapped my friend upon the back", and, suiting the action to the words, gave my brother a resounding slap on the back. Will was rather frail, and it nearly knocked him off the piano stool.

While at the Royal College of Music he often amused himself making pen drawings of some of the students and staff, which were so well thought of that my father was advised that he might do even better in art. But it also appears that at the time he entered the Royal College or Music a number of his drawings were submitted to the Royal Academy (Schools?), and that the president (presumably Leighton) had pronounced against them because they tended towards caricature. He drew alphabet people, village scenes, and occasionally "nigger" boys. He once drew some of these "nigger" boys on a tea cloth at the home of some friends in London, for the ladies later to pick out in silk. I can remember him drawing for us quite a lot, and in particular Stan asking him on one occasion to draw a horse for him.

The influential names of those days, the Ansons, the Coleridges, the Purnells and the Youngs, which had become a part of the early Fernley life, very largely vanished soon after our births. To us our parents showed little inclination to talk about these interesting and exciting times. It was only as we grew more into the family that we began to recognise the difference between those days and our present situation. The piano presented by the Prince of Wales to Will bore no indication of its donor; his successes with Harold at their recitals in London were far away; his drawings which Stan had so much admired lay rolled up behind the books in the bookcase until we found them again.

True enough, the clock presented to my father still stood on the mantelpiece in the dining-room, bearing its engraved plate. But all the time we were at home it was never going; my father would declare that it had a sensitive spring.

Yet my father's nose for patrons was always wonderfully keen, and he followed this star more or less all his life. The Duke of Westminster and Mr. Beaumont, to name only two, sent Will and Harold to the Royal College of Music; and later Lady Boston was the sponsor when Stan went to the Slade.

But Father was not so successful in other ways, and the stories we heard later about our elder brothers' early training made us thankful that we were following a profession he knew nothing about. It may have been ambition or it may have been over-anxiety, but he drove Will to such long hours of practice, and in order to protect his hands allowed him to take so little a part in games, that ultimately Will's health was seriously undermined and for a time he had to be kept in a highly expensive nursing home in the country—for which no patron was forthcoming.

I always regarded Father as of a despondent temperament, and his efforts to rectify matters at this time went to show how impractical he could be. Now he flung away the fruits of painfully acquired educations for jobs at half-crown a week.

His sense of detachment may have helped him but it threw the burden of getting things right on to my mother's shoulders. It was she who decided that the extremely expensive place to which Willie had been sent, and which was diminishing our resources, had too much the appearance of a club for rich dilettantes with a turn for discussion and a belief that they had been reprieved from facing life outside. And so with persistence she eventually got him back to Cookham. Later he was able to give further recitals in London, and finally he married and took a post at the Cologne Conservatoire. But the family never fully recovered from the heavy burdens then incurred.

It was into this confusion of ambitions, high endeavour, disappointments and partial recovery that Stanley and I were born.

My sister Annie had to act as our nurse. The last of the professional nurses had left, but more Spencers kept on arriving, and it is small wonder that Annie should have stamped her foot when I was born.

In the nursery, which was not large, there was a double bed, with an iron cot on either side. The furniture was simple and for practical purposes only, and the floor was bare boards. Two pictures only hung on the walls—"The Bengal Lancer" and one of a sailor and his lass sitting on a wall gazing out on to a very rough sea.

When they were at home the large bed was occupied by Horace and Sydney, while Stan and I each had a crib. The bars in mine appeared to have been bent at some time—and so they had. Either Will or Harold—family tradition fluctuated—got his head through and could not get it out, and so my father had sent for the blacksmith, who arrived looking like Vulcan with his leather apron and clanging iron tools, while my brother's head continued to wriggle the wrong side of the bars until he was released.

We were washed when put to bed, and our hair, which my mother insisted on keeping long for years beyond the time when any self-respecting boy should have had his hair cut short, was put up in curlers which Annie used to make by tearing newspapers into strips. They were most uncomfortable and kept us awake. (But there were other things as well to do this.)

At a suitable age we began saying prayers dictated by Annie, simple to begin with but complicated later by the addition of an ever-increasing postscript, as more and more unknown relations died or got into other difficulties—what the fate of dear Aunt Emma was, Stan and I never knew.

The formalities which might be expected to follow going to bed—the blowing out of the lamp (in this instance a rather smoky flame which had its existence at the top of what looked like a misshapen lemonade bottle), the drawing of the curtains (a red and white striped blind), the lighting of the night light (a continuation of the smoky flame on top of the bottle), and finally the creeping out of

ANNIE PRACTISING AFTER PUTTING US TO BED

the room to the dying accompaniment of soft lullabies—none of this ever happened to us. Having put us down, Annie, who was a member of the Maidenhead Orchestral Society, would then prop her music up on the chest of drawers and by the aid of the same smoky lamp would practise her viola, while Stan and I would follow the shadow of her bow up the wall across the ceiling and back again.

Downstairs in the dining-room, which was directly below the nursery, my father would continue to receive pupils till long after our supposed time for going to sleep. Some of the pupils could not come at any other time, because their businesses and shops detained them; and one gentleman would bring along with his powerful bass voice a song composed and published by my brother Harold, entitled "Give a man a horse he can ride". So in addition to Annie's viola, our lullabies might include Handel, Beethoven, Schubert or Mozart, and occasionally my father's voice: "You play the piano like one of your father's cart horses."

But finally Father would have got rid of his last pupil downstairs, the lamp would have been drawn over to his side of the table, and opening a book he would read into the small hours of the morning, and we would go to sleep.

There were nightmares. As a family we were prone to them, and Stan and I would occasionally share one; but I have felt since that the chance of being carried into our parents' bed may have influenced us. An overwhelming sense of security would follow this, and if we woke up next morning to find ourselves back in our cots, we had no sense of being misled or cheated.

With the morning the day started as it would in most nurseries. Annie got us up and we would go down to breakfast—a very simple meal indeed—after which we returned to the nursery where, if it was wet, we had to remain. There was not a lot to amuse us there; the toys were scarce and often had been passed on. An early example of a jig-saw puzzle, of a faded pink colour, proved on completion to be a map of the Crimea. There was a tin full of buttons of all shapes and sizes, some which might have done service at the time of the Crimea or even Waterloo. These two examples of nursery entertainment were probably brought over from Vine Cottage.

There was not a lot besides, and one gets a fairly vivid picture of the nursery life of that time and before through one of Mother's recollections—of a rumpus in the nursery between Percy and Horace. When she intervened, Horace explained to her that he could find no justification for Percy's dissatisfaction with his share, as he had given him the chest of drawers to play with!

There was a notable day when Stan broke the chamber pot. I can remember my brother Willie, in his frock coat, leading him off to Mother: "Mother, Stanley has come to confess." There was no pledge to sign this time, but the Slack characteristics were as strong in Willie as they were in Stan.

As I have said, the floor was bare, and we played on it with what we had: the puzzle, the buttons, and later a box of bricks. But this scarcity of toys started us off on our own account. Cutting out abstract paper patterns was good value, and this later spread to paper nuns. How those nuns ever got into the nursery through the barrage of non-conformity downstairs is one of the deeper mysteries, but we processed them all round the room.

We were kept quite happy up there, with Annie in regular attendance, and as we grew older we liked more and more making our own toys rather than having "real" ones. When Stan did get a "real" one from Lord Boston's Christmas tree, which proved to be a doll, he smashed its head off on the end of the bed.

If the day continued wet, we remained in the nursery. It was our world on wet days and outside became the universe. Certainly there were hidden bits of Cookham as remote as the Milky Way, and they remained so.

The pupils were coming all day, and we derived what amusement and interest we could by sometimes watching them from the window. Listening to the music was no longer a conscious process; it had become as much a part of our lives as breathing. And the life of the school next door gave us patches of amusement when the children came out to play.

It was no use blowing bubbles when it rained, but their disappearance and re-appearance far away over the fir tree or over the Malt House wall was a fair weather thrill. The three rather gaunt pinnacles of the Malt House reared themselves up to heaven. Any of them could have passed for the Tower of Babel, and Mr. Sandalls and the others up there mending them could have been the victims of the Almighty's frustrating trick.

THE BOX OF BUTTONS

If they were gaunt when seen in daylight, their shadowy shapes became frightening by night, as very little could be seen except for one window in the furnace room, which glowed red and against which the shadow of a man passed from time to time to stoke up the fire—enough to give us plenty of nightmares if Annie forgot to pull down the blind.

Round about tea time, in the fading light, we would gravitate towards the fire. It was protected by a guard which was more easily taken off than put on, but Annie was always there. Having lit the lamp she would read to us. At this time the library downstairs would have been very largely for the use of the grown-ups, and to prepare us for it my father on his "London days" always purchased one of W. T. Stead's "Books for the Bairns", published at 1d.

It was through them and Annie that we early got a smattering of good English. There was Brer Rabbit, Snow White (which moved us almost to tears), *Don Quixote*, *Gulliver's Travels*, *Pilgrim's Progress*, *Tanglewood Tales*, and the adventures of that fantastic figure, Baron Munchausen. Many of them were illustrated; the lively drawings by Brinsley Le Fanu for Brer Rabbit had a great influence.

We were healthy children. In the family recollections there was very little reference to illness, and when there was, it was generally because there was a good story attached. We only knew that my sister Florence had been ill because of the comment of our servant of that time, Mildred, while sitting with her, "Lor, Miss Florence, what a lovely corpse you'd make".

However critical illnesses had been in the past, they had become very light-hearted affairs by the time our turn came round. One or other of us would become drowsy, Mother would put her hand on us and say: "Feverish," and to bed we would go, with hot bread-and-milk and demerara sugar Dr. Plum would be sent for. Once he diagnosed measles, and added: "Put 'em all in one room together, Mrs. Spencer," and as many Spencers as were available at the time got measles. For our amusement when recovering, my mother fixed up a string contraption by which we could pass messages from one room to another. We also had crayons and drawing books, and occasionally transfers.

But when Horace went down with scarlet fever it was taken much more seriously. Father was banished from the house, the school was closed, and we were shooed out of the nursery and found alternative accommodation with the other members of the household, servants and all. I think Stan and I were sleeping in the nursery with Horace the night before Dr. Plum diagnosed scarlet fever. A sheet soaked in carbolic was then hung outside the nursery door to protect us from contagion, and it did. We all moved about the rest of the house and we all escaped. Mother did all the nursing and continued to run the house as well. When Horace was convalescing, she shut him up in the nursery, ordered wood from Mr. Wiggs, and with hammer, saw, chisels and nails set Horace to work to make a cabinet, to keep him busy and happy. We were very frightened when she finally entered the room to set off the sulphur candles, and feared she might not get out in time.

In fair weather the skies of Cookham were bright and strong, and against this the old red-brick cottages and the colour-washed houses gave a cheerful welcome to visitors entering the village from the moor.

The lanes round the village were well shaded by elm trees, while here and there a high wall would conceal either one of Grandpa's ugly houses or some fine old lodge. Surrounded as the village was with commons, meadows, streams, ditches and backwaters, and curtained off on its eastern fringe by the lofty ridge of Cliveden Woods high above the cottages, it would have been the toll gate that finally contributed to our feeling of being islanders.

Many of the houses were mysteries to us, largely hidden as they were behind these walls and trees. But occasionally gates were left open, and we got opportunities to see inside. Robert Louis Stevenson describes swinging high into other lands, and we, by climbing the fir tree in the garden, used to get the same sensation; the thrill of seeing bits of Cookham cropping up in strange places so unexpectedly never lost its charm for us.

We did not like going to other places to stay. In fact, I only remember one occasion when we did go, to stay with my brother Harold and his wife Natalie at Furz Platt, Maidenhead, and we hated it. There was nothing of Cookham there. A man playing a mouth organ passing through a cornfield near the house compared very badly with the lovely sounds of stringed instruments coming over to us from the King's Arms lawn, which was such a feature of any fine summer evening at Cookham. And pavements! Street lighting!! A gas oven!!! All contributed to a severe attack of homesickness, and it was a great relief to us when Annie walked over from Cookham and took us home. We had only stayed one night.

Stan and I wore straw sailor hats in the summer. Although I do not now remember the ships' names emblazoned on them, I am sure one of them must have been *Dreadnought*. They were very uncomfortable to wear, being held on our heads by a piece of elastic that was too tight. But as a family we were not in favour of the jingo sentiments of those times.

When passing ladies of the village we were expected to lift our hats. It was one of the disciplines of our upbringing, but, having regard to the effort involved, the responses we got were very disappointing, amounting to little more than a nod. The hats got severely damaged in what can only be described as the debacle of trying to get them off in time. In the circumstances, it was left to Annie to devise a scheme by which the hats could be preserved and the painful effects of the elastic could be avoided.

Anyone taking a walk along the footpath by Barley Hill might have come on us practising a series of movements by which we were able to get clear of our hats in time: I. Remove elastic from under chin. II. Lift hat. III. Replace hat on head. IV. Replace elastic under chin. But even so, if we came unexpectedly on someone round a corner, it was only due to the excellence of the drilling we received from Annie that further disasters were averted.

At dusk, looking up the village towards the moor, the fire from the blacksmith's shop would send a warm shaft of light across the road to the cottages on the other side. It would flicker as Mr. Johnson or Mr. Gibbs, the blacksmiths, damped down the fire for the night, and finally disappear as Fred Duckett, who worked there, came out and lifted up the heavy shutters to close the shop.

There was not a lot that poor Fred could do. We were told that his condition—he was an imbecile—was caused by his father having turned him upside down when he was a child. But he could make himself useful in some ways. He could lead the less spirited and the tired horses back to their owners after they had been shod. He could be relied on to carry messages. Both Mr. Gibbs and Mr. Johnson were very kind to him. Occasionally he was teased, but that was heavily frowned on. With Stan and me he was a regular member of the congregation at Chapel.

For much of the day it might be thought that he was not in the smithy at all, but he was there, hidden away in the darkness behind the chimney working the bellows. Occasionally the fire would erupt like a miniature Vesuvius—a pretty sight with sparks flying all around—and at these moments the apparition of Fred would emerge, and he too would flicker up, and fade again as the fire was damped down again.

When Annie took us for a walk, she might get well towards the Fleet Bridge before noticing that we were no longer with her. And it was being left behind by Annie that brought Stan and me together in print for the first time, although not by name.

In summer time a regular visitor had been the novelist Douglas Sladen. He could not fail to come under our notice on account of his appearance. He wore a light alpaca suit, a very large panama hat, and what appeared to be black sun glasses. He was always accompanied by his secretary, to whom he dictated his novels as they walked around the village. We were told that in one of them—in what context we never knew—he described two little boys who were always calling after their nurse, "Wait for me, Annie. Oh, Annie, wait for us."

With heavy rains beating against the nursery windows, driven there by boisterous south-west winds, and with much talk downstairs about floods, there were times when our thoughts inevitably turned to the story of the great Cookham flood, when there were boats in the village street. An old photograph exists of a punt entering the Royal Exchange through the front door. Bread, we were told, was delivered on the ends of poles from boats to cottagers marooned in their bedrooms. All this made us the more eager to see a flood for ourselves.

The floods always came quicker than they went. Our walks would become more and more curtailed, and our excitement would rise with the waters.

The moor, instead of looking its usual self, was now gone, or was fast disappearing; so were the marsh meadows. Where was the river now? There was Cookham Bridge, but looking strangely out of place.

Towards evening, looking up the village, a group of men might be seen silhouetted against the water, contemplating it thoughtfully. Occasionally one would turn and look down the village.

The posts at the entry to the causeway were removed so that a certain amount of wheeled traffic could use it, and those that marked the road now revealed to us what they were really there for. As darkness fell, the bus and one or two cabs could be seen, the horses with the water up to their bellies, ploughing their way along it back to the village.

A brief conversation between the driver and Mr. Keeley, the keeper of the common, and trestles were brought out and put in position, and scaffold poles were placed against them, on which red hurricane lamps were hung. In the darkness the red gleam from these lamps conveyed the message to us that Cookham was now cut off from the outer world.

The next morning when we went out the transformation was complete. The village and everything about it was now

FLOODS ON COOKHAM MOOR

a mass of confusing reflections. Bits of the village, upside down and miles below our feet, brought a new fascination to our walks. The sticks we had stuck in the ground at the edge of the water were going out to "sea". But when they started coming inland again, and the scaffold poles were lifted and the hurricane lamps taken down, we knew that there would be no boats in Cookham village this time, and were very sorry.

This sheltered life of ours, of the nursery and the walks with Annie, continued for a long time. Being read to by Annie, and the interests we made for ourselves, kept us happy enough. I was making models of farms and farm carts, and Stan was drawing a lot more. Some of the drawings were of rather an odd nature. There was one of Cookham Fire Brigade riding on snails on the cobbled stones in front of the Bell and Dragon Hotel, worked in black and red ink, in which the drawing of the firemen with their helmets and uniforms was a miracle. This work of his was seriously intended, and should not be regarded as frivolous. Even at this early date, without perhaps being very aware of it, he had, I think, joined issue with his destiny.

Percy would bring in branches from the fir tree and tie them to the end of the bed, and Stan would cut out some of his little figures and conceal them among the branches and entertain himself looking through at them.

That this sort of thing could not continue for ever was of course apparent to everyone except Stan and me. The first signs of things to come did not trouble us. After all, pot-hooks and hangers in the nursery amused us—provided they did not go on for too long. We learnt our alphabet in a reasonable time; I don't remember our nursing any objection to it. And if later Annie showed us how to put letters together to make words, what was the matter with that? None of this interfered with my farms and Stan's drawings. Nor did the figures with dots round them. But our education had commenced.

So often it happens that when changes take place they do so in ways beyond the control of those most deeply affected.

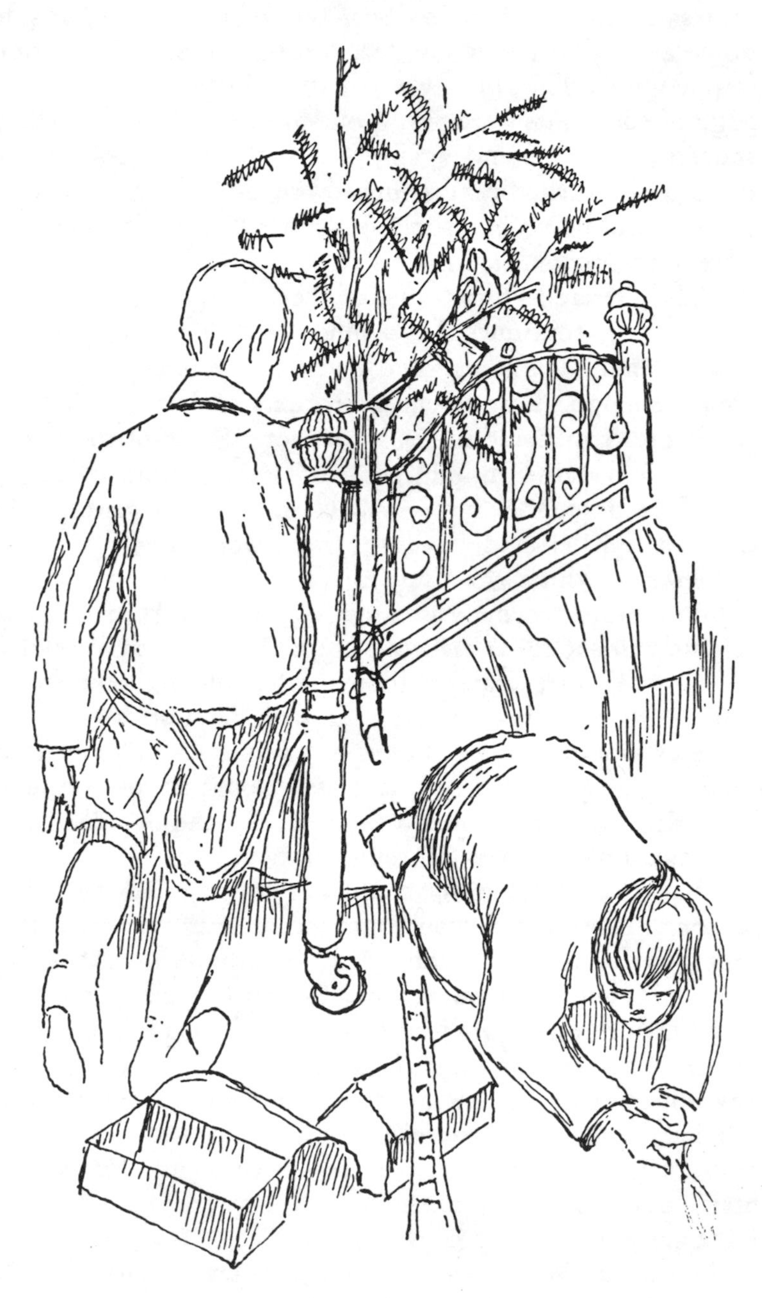

STAN AND THE BRANCH FROM THE FIR TREE

Stan and I were quite prepared to continue as we were, but the two Miss Georges were not, and the amusement we derived by looking out of the window at the school received a severe setback when they gave the school up and went to Australia.

As things turned out, their decision softened the blow of change for us. When one thinks of the effect that going to school for the first time has on most children, how lucky we were: all we had to do was to transfer our nursery down the path into the school with Annie and Florence, who took it over.

But there was a problem. Stan and I had to be told that the interests and discipline of the school demanded that while Annie and Florence could still be Annie and Florence at home, and might continue so down the path, the moment we were in the school they each had to become Miss Spencer. Sometimes, if Stan and I slipped up and said "Annie", or worse still "Flo", we would look at one another and hope it had not been noticed.

In those days, private schools could run along quite happily without curricula, reports and Parents' Days; and classes would depend on the number of pupils. If there were not enough pupils to make up classes, which was so in our case, then individual attention was the order of the day; and perhaps that was just as well, as the pupils were more remarkable for their personalities than their scholarship. For instance, Jack Hatch would graciously make this concession to my sister: "Alright, Miss, I'll say buckit in school, but it will always be buckert out."

Discipline was maintained by occasional reference to Father, who could be heard giving lessons to his pupils indoors: he was a kind of threat held over our heads, and this prompted Hilda Jemmet to ask if "that was what he was kept for".

Hilda was regarded by us as something of a mystery. Parentless and dressed in black, she lodged at Cookham Rise. One day she took everyone completely by surprise, including my father, by bringing to school a sheaf of poems; Father and Will spent much time searching among their books, Keats especially, to trace their origin.

But our education at our first school still left plenty of leeway to be made up, if we were going to be prepared for later life. If the whole of our mathematics was not culled from the back of our exercise books, what was there was a great aid. Nouns, verbs, adjectives, pronouns and adverbs seemed about all there was in Grammar. Spelling we learnt by mistakes. We worked on slates quite a lot and a sponge was provided for cleaning. We did our drawing in printed drawing books. On one half of the sheet there would be a portrait of Roman Emperor or Gladiator and we had to copy it on the other half. There was some natural history; wild flowers were brought in by the pupils. French was "without tears", and probably without much accuracy of pronunciation either. Boadicea, Julius Caesar, William the Conqueror and a few others found a place in history. It was all very elementary, but in many ways it was the best kind of schooling as preparation for careers in which individuality was going to be the mainspring.

It might not have suited everyone. Many years later I was told that one of the pupils, who had joined the police force, failed to gain promotion because his arithmetic was weak. But a school which could produce two L.R.C.M.s, two R.A.s, a conjuror and a policeman had an interesting if unusual honours board.

Although the other children did not go out for walks, we continued to do so with Annie, and it was on these walks that we would occasionally come upon William Bailey, on the fringes of Odney Common or the moor, painting his pictures. He was a most excellent Sunday painter. He painted willow trees in sepia washes—two of them flanked an engraving of Turner's approach to Venice in the dining-room. He painted a lovely watery atmospheric oil of Cookham Bridge and used to talk of the "lost-and-foundness of things". If his influence on us was mainly subconscious, it took positive form when his daughter, Dorothy Bailey, herself an artist and designer, took us in hand and gave us our first lessons in painting. For these we used to go over to her house. The lessons we had were very simple and direct, and these visits gave us further opportunities of seeing Mr. Bailey's work, many examples of which hung in the drawing-room, augmented by works by David Murray and Amonia, both of whom he knew.

I think Mother was more watchful at this time about the last members of her family than Father was. The books and crayons to draw with, when we were ill in bed, were the natural expedient of any mother with sick children and a lot of work to do. But it was she, I can remember, who drew Father's attention to some drawings which Stan had done of Bunyan's Vanity Fair.

She asked me to go on with my piano practice, but Annie, who could play the piano, up to Clementi and Dussek, as well as the viola, was too tired to be an interested teacher any more.

As we grew a little older, we became more a part of the family downstairs and less of the nursery. In the nursery Annie no longer dictated our prayers; we said them to ourselves, and Aunt Emma and a few others got left out.

We could now read well enough, for the books which were being given us included Hans Andersen's Fairy Tales, *Oliver Twist*, and *Mr. Sponge's Sporting Tour*, and we now read the Bible by a card-index system of dates and portions to be read. But we were still in Annie's charge, and although the school was now virtually closed, a desultory education continued downstairs in the dining-room, out of which we would be turned when music pupils came—but these were not so plentiful—and to which we returned after they had gone; and then Father would take a hand too.

But before we moved out of the nursery a sparrow hawk moved in. Now when we went to bed there was no longer Annie's bow to follow round the room. But instead, one night we found ourselves sitting bolt upright with our eyes fixed on the apparition of a bird perched on a soap box at the end of the bed, with a hood over its head and two holes for its eyes. Then away downstairs we could hear a muffled voice crying "Ho-eek, ho-eek", and the wretched bird started a kind of curtseying in our direction. As the "ho-eeking" became nearer and more audible, the bird got more excited and we got more frightened, until at last Horace entered carrying a plate of raw beef cut into thin strips which he proceeded to threddle down the bird's throat.

It was my mother's idea; she had heard Horace express a wish to become a falconer, and with her the word had only to be on Horace's lips to bring her into action.

We were getting older, but we were not old enough for this kind of palaver every night, and I doubt if we were very sorry when the butcher, by mistake, gave Horace salt beef and the bird died, and the idea of Horace becoming a falconer died with it.

CHAPTER III

NOW THAT WE were getting away from the nursery, and moving about with greater freedom, we saw more of Mother, and we began to realise how much she worked about the house, helped by our faithful servant, Alice. She was a very active woman and undertook all manner of tasks. She papered the dining-room and passage in the days of the "dado"—and was at great pains to get it straight. The designs of the paper were brown and ugly, but that was not her fault. They were governed by the prevailing fashions. But she was quite uncritical about it, as were we all. She, like Stan, was small and she was not strong, but given the opportunity she would take on the ceiling as well.

She was never puzzled or put out by her family, however difficult they may have been at times. They were her children and she was their mother—strong willed and strong minded, without a semblance of weakness. She knew and must have practised the arts of silence and timely intervention to perfection, to have controlled and directed us as she did, and to have kept everything going as she did.

Father made his presence felt too, but less so than Mother. His role was of course a different one, and he was away visiting his pupils much of the time. We noticed that his way of resting differed from my mother's. She never slept, or attempted to do so, until she went to bed. In the afternoons she rested on the sofa in the dining-room, where she read Emerson. Father, on the other hand, would take what he called his "forty winks" after dinner, and to stimulate this he would place his napkin over his face.

Occasionally we were allowed to leave the nursery earlier than usual if Annie had had to go out before our time for coming downstairs. When this happened we ran about the house amusing ourselves—no doubt at times getting in and out of Mother's and Alice's way. Seated on the kitchen doorstep one morning, my Mother overheard me ask Stan what angels were. "Great white birds what pecks" he replied, and to my further enquiry as to whether Annie was one, he added: "No, not great whopping things like her." On another occasion, when we had selected the front doorstep, this brought us into contact with Mr. Goldsmith, the piano tuner. Seeing us there he observed to Stan: "Hullo, my boy, you don't look very fat, what do you have for dinner?" When my Mother overheard Stan's reply, "Brembutter pudding and not much of that," she was deeply disturbed.

And what was now happening in the passage by the front door must have been, besides a cause for some anxiety, an embarrassment as well. We had started to eat the wall. We did not eat it for something to do, neither did we eat it because we were hungry, we ate it because we liked it. It was a laborious task, necessitating stripping off the paper to get at the crumbling cement. Dr. Plum was consulted and attributed it to an absence of lime in our systems. Whether this was so or not, we could not go on eating the house, and mustard was spread on the wall to stop us. We were still seldom allowed to sit up for supper.

Back in the nursery our amusements, advancing a little, were finding new directions. The box of buttons and the puzzle no longer interested us. Among our books, Brer Rabbit with the Le Fanu illustrations was still a favourite, but Stan was heard now to express a wish to draw like Arthur Rackham. His drawing was for a long time not seriously regarded. There was no strong interest in pictures at home. They were the least discussed topic, and what was on the walls was a fair indication of the level of taste. It was still possible for my sister Florence to ask me, in preference to Stan, to paint a little picture for Mother's birthday present. But when, after the Cookham Fire Brigade drawing, came the Vanity Fair drawings, with their powerful characterisations, they did, as I've said, attract Mother. Bunyan had certainly captured his imagination. Yet there was nothing precocious about him. And he was not understood: when he stuck the photograph of a pig's head over the face of a brother in the family album, it was regarded as merely unkind. I failed, too, to comprehend his avid interest in his drawing, though when on one occasion I threw a pen at him, which stuck in his forehead, I was perhaps doing no more than any child might do when he and his brother both wanted the same thing.

The entertainments in the village were not of a particularly high standard and we did not often attend. Had stardom existed in those days, then unquestionably the honours would have gone to Paul Pym and his Pierrettes. Our social life was still so much restricted to our life at home that when we did go to any parties, we were shy and nervous, but we attended some of these performances. When we were about ten and eleven respectively, we became members of the Young Helpers League, which aimed at raising funds for Dr. Barnardo's Homes. We had a collecting box and through this we were able to understand the plight of and extend our sympathies towards the unfortunate little children so feelingly depicted on it. But now these sympathies were going to be extended in another direction by a proposal from the local organising secretary, Miss Lucy Taylor, a bustling, never-take-no-for-an-answer type of woman, that we should take part in an entertainment.

In the village our shyness or nervousness had been remarked on, and there were occasions when one or two of the neighbours, to bring us out a little more, took us to Maidenhead, once for a drive and to tea and on another occasion by train. If the intention of Miss Taylor's proposal had been to entertain the villagers, at home I don't believe any such considerations entered anyone's head. It was received as something more in the nature of a challenge or a test. We had no say in the matter. It was a miserable piece of doggerel we had to sing, and none of the hoped-for results materialised; but our failure seemed to have put the audience into a happy frame of mind and we received an ovation for other reasons. There was another occasion when Father decided to give a concert at Hedsor in aid of charity, and for this the whole family was marshalled—piano, fiddle, viola, singing, conjuring. This time Stan and I had to sing a dull duet called "Pickles", but rehearsing was now a much more serious matter. Father was sponsoring this concert, which gave it an air of professionalism; and to bring us up to concert pitch, he rehearsed us himself. And he trained us as earnestly as he rehearsed my brother Will, who was practising a fairly hefty piece of Chopin for the concert. We differed only in the amount of time expended. With Father at the helm, there was going to be no repetition of the unprofessional success we had had with "When Father laid the Carpet on the Stairs". Father's own contribution was a little sketch which he wrote, and in which Stan and I joined him. The only member of the family in the audience was my Mother.

Christmas had a great appeal for us, as for all children. Our approach to it was simple. We were then accepting the Bible uncritically—the Creation, Noah and the Flood, the crossing of the Red Sea, the Tower of Babel; so that the laying of Jesus in the manger presented us with no problems, and had anyone raised any they would have been frowned upon. We would have answered the challenge with a degree of finality—"cos so". A Fernley Christmas Eve was a Bible affair, without the Bible necessarily being opened at all. My Father's Bible habit could bring that simple narrative to life in other ways if he wished. Stan and I could well imagine that the Shepherds watching their flocks would have been in the field below Cliveden Woods. That was the land of the Nativity for us.

If the whole festival of Christmas could have continued in the spirit of Christmas Eve, if that spirit of anticipation could have remained, we would have been well pleased. The carol singers would arrive at our back door, and even if it was not very good singing, it had a rough and ready honesty about it which was liked; some would have gone so far as to say that it was in the true spirit of Christmas. Then we were content to go to bed and listen to the sound of the bells and of the villagers in the street below on their way to the service in Cookham Church, lit by candlelight, at midnight. For us it was largely a nocturnal event; perhaps a little mixed with our feelings of mystery as to what went on downstairs after we had gone to bed.

With Christmas morning the mood changed. As very young children we had reached disillusioning knowledge of the Christmas stocking, a gauzy mass-produced affair which we had seen on our walks, hanging amidst cotton wool and tinsel in Mr. Buckham's shop. We awoke not to a stocking but to a situation of urgency and bustle. My Father and Will ate a hurried breakfast; they had to get away to their organs at Hedsor and Cores End Congregational Chapel. Almost immediately they were followed by the strong-armed Alice carrying the turkey, covered by a napkin, to the bakehouse to be roasted. For Mother and Alice it was a hard day.

It was the custom for as many as could to go to church on Christmas morning even though Stan and I were supposed to be chapel; and we would arrive only just in time to avoid being cut off from what was always regarded as our pew by the choir processing round the church. If, as occasionally was the case, we found strangers with us in our pew, we were embarrassed because we had never familiarised ourselves sufficiently with the Prayer Book to avoid having to be shown our places by Annie, and we might still turn over at the wrong time. The services at church were so low that our parents did not mind mixing Church and Chapel together for us. This may give point to a comment of my brother to me many years later: that, if only people knew, through his pictures it was "Cookham Church at one end and Cookham Chapel at the other". But the mixing was all within well-defined limits.

For dinner, an extra leaf (which was kept in the cupboard for the rest of the year) was added to the table. Mother took her place at its head, and except that Father always said Grace and was served first, there were no other indications that he was not one of us. Later, visiting other homes in the village, we realised that this was a habit of the times.

If the walks after dinner were intended as constitutionals, they also occasionally revived some of the Christmas Eve spirit. Coming to Pound Farm at the bottom of Terrys Lane as evening approached, seeing the cowmen still at work, their hurricane lamps lighting up each cow in turn as they moved around whistling, and hearing the sound of buckets and milk cans, brought back something of the pastoral atmosphere until, returning across the moor home for tea, we left all this behind again.

Another Victorianism which was maintained at home was the sanctity of the drawing-room. It was seldom used, but we always had tea there on Christmas Day. Unhappily, the room faced north, and having been left unused for such long periods it was damp and cold. A heavy green curtain hung in front of the door to stop the draughts. The furnishing of the room was muddled Edwardian, which meant that Victoria had not yet been ousted. Wickerwork chairs draped with muslin, caught up with ribbons, tied in bows, shared the seating arrangements with something near-Empire—upholstered chairs which were very uncomfortable. But Stan and I would of course be on the floor, probably building houses with old playing cards given us by our Uncle Julius, or perhaps engaged in ludo.

A grand piano swallowed up much of the room, and owing to the dampness and to the fact that fires were seldom lit, it was in very bad condition. The mantelpiece had a large and ornate mirror over it, and standing on the mantelpiece in front of it was a remarkable clock, all gilded over and protected by a glass dome. It was a military masterpiece. A drum formed the clock, and on each side, in heroic pose, stood a grenadier of the time of the Crimea and what looked like a sepoy. There were flags and rifles and a piece of artillery as well. It was indeed a skilful piece of metal work. It suffered the same fault as the clock in the dining-room, but was more interesting to look at. There were glass candlesticks, which were not used, and knick-knacks were

THE COWMAN AT MOOR FARM

dotted about the room, little china figures and china swans which floated round central flower vases. The lace curtains against the Venetian blinds added to the lacy effect of the room as a whole.

There was an excellent little oil painting by Amonia, of some water lilies, next to which was an overbearing reproduction of Millais' Ophelia, which in our childhood used to frighten us. In the darkened corner above the piano was a large engraving of the head of Carlyle, and among other choices made by my Mother at different times was a large and meticulous water colour of the River and Cookham Church by William Bradley.

After tea, and the freezing we got in the drawing-room, we were glad to get back to the warmth of the dining-room where free-for-all developed till supper time. There was scope for entertainment, but the difficulty now was to find not the artists but the audience. However, Stan and I were able to fill this role, as at this time our only interventions had not been very goód. We sang carols; Father played the Harmonious Blacksmith with the keyboard covered by a cloth; Percy sang; Horace produced cards out of Father's coat-tail pocket and other beautifully performed tricks; Harold played Handel's Water Music, into which he wove the blasts of the boats' sirens going up and down the river. Mother and Alice joined in the carols as they threaded themselves among us, getting the supper. Alice always joined us for this meal.

After it, before leaving the table, there was a ceremonial trial of my Father for his misdeeds during the year. For these trials Harold would assume the role of Judge and Prosecutor, placing his napkin on top of his head as a wig. He would proceed to confront Father with, for instance, the offence of throwing "Sordello" down on the table in a state of irritation, declaring that he could not understand a word of it. Out of such charges, Harold would weave an intriguing and insinuating summing-up, with his eyes fixed on Father the whole time. Father seemed to enjoy it all thoroughly.

When the trial was over, the table was cleared and pushed to one end of the room, and as much furniture as possible was cleared into the passage. Stan and I would sit on top of the table—it was rather like being in the gallery—while my Father and Mother and the rest of the family sat below. At some undetectable signal, Harold, who had now taken his seat at the piano, would strike up a tarantella, and a Spanish ballerina in a flaming red dress, with castanets and a mane of flowing black hair, who had been hiding outside for her cue, would hurtle in like a ball of fire and go whirling round the room until, as the music ended, she ended with a graceful bow and we could see that it was Natalie.

With what time there was left we played Up Jenkins and Old Maid, and with a final carol, or perhaps a reading by Father from *A Christmas Carol* or *The Ingoldsby Legends*, we would be off to bed, leaving him to draw the lamp over to his side of the table, and settle down as usual with his book and a cigar, which, if its life was nearing its end, he would prolong by impaling it on the end of his penknife.

As far as it concerned us, Boxing Day had little to offer. If there were parties, very few came our way, but on the whole we were happier for this. There were no children's parties for us at home, by which to learn the technique. Oranges and Lemons had worn thin at home before our time. We had to tag along as best we could with our elders.

The only event which comes to mind that took place on a Boxing Day was when we joined forces with Uncle Julius and family, and together walked as far as Winter Hill and back. Cockmarsh Hill lay on our track and from this vantage point we could observe a pigeon shoot taking place at the farm below. Every time a pigeon got away we expressed our approval by clapping. But we were not fanatically opposed to shooting. Father could relish the annual brace of pheasants from Lord Boston, and I seem to remember a conversation about pheasants being nourishing food.

When recently I revisited Fernley, I was astonished at how small it now seemed. As children we all seemed to have enough elbow room, and did so much there. But of course

NATALIE DANCING

there were seldom more than five of us at home at one time except for special occasions. That my Father was said to be, and in fact was, irritable at times would seem to have been inevitable in the circumstances. There was always the sound of music in the little house. Willie and Harold, Annie, Florence, Percy and Sydney, and later myself, had all been allowed to attempt (even if we did not necessarily wish it) one instrument or another: piano, violin, viola, 'cello. And as a kind of secondary fire-ball to Natalie, there was always Horace's conjuring, and at times other activities of which he had less experience, with which to gear up life at home.

Cookham continued in her peaceful way, the smoke from the cottage chimneys curled up to the blue sky, the stillness made itself felt. We mostly preferred the autumn and winter. The strong tonal contrasts of the village with its surrounding fields and commons and over-hanging woods, and here and there the flashes of the white waters of the Fleet or the Strand, sharpened the scene for us.

Now Stan was finding his way more frequently to the front bedroom after tea. There, lighting his candle, he would either read his large Bible or John Donne, or he would draw out some idea. Sepia washes and pencil were his favourite medium from the start, and often he reinforced them with Indian ink. I have always thought that "Amy Hatch Feeding the Motherless Calf" was his earliest composition—as distinct from his early illustrations and drawings round the village. I think he was at the Technical School at Maidenhead when he did it.

Occasionally he would slip downstairs when Father went out, to pick his way through some Bach on the piano, while for me the "after tea feeling", which was such a favoured period for Stan upstairs, would send me edging my way to one end of the kitchen table while Alice, perched at the other end, was reading. Here I continued very happily sand-papering and painting my models. Sometimes I wanted tin, and a row of empty red, white and blue coffee tins on top of the dresser were to hand. At other times, I wanted leather with which to make the harness for my extraordinary horses, and this was also to hand behind the dresser curtain, where there were rows upon rows of old boots and shoes spanning the whole life of Fernley. For colouring the carts Stan would let me have some of his paints. One or two of the villagers, who sometimes encouraged me by giving a shilling for one of them, will, if still living, be interested in the fact that some of the colours with which I painted them came from the palette he was using for Elizabeth and Zacharias and other pictures of that time. If he was finding conditions at home at all disturbing, there was no evidence of it either in his demeanour or his work.

He and Sydney would often speak of John Donne and *Urn Burial*, and had I been of a literary turn of mind I could have absorbed much from them. But I was not, and thus failed to connect what he was reading with his burial of a box with a drawing in it down Mill Lane.

Looking back at this boyhood period, I don't think that it would be true to regard him in so simple a light as some have done. At an early age to have been called a "little spitfire"; to have been called "tiger" out in the village; to have covered the face of a brother in the family photograph album with a pig's head; to have deeply interested himself in the flow of blood from a cut in the arm of another brother; to have left the imprint of his boot on the shin of another villager; to be very quick to lose his temper; to defy authority at the age of twelve by tearing up a note with which Annie had despatched him to Father, complaining of his behaviour, and to announce defiantly that he had done so on returning to the schoolroom—all this was another aspect of my almost twin brother.

What I have just written could be a criticism, or it could be something else. I am pretty sure that when I threw the pen at him and it stuck in his forehead, it was an act of retaliation, and a protest against moments when to all intents and purposes he would seem overbearing. But in point of fact it was a matter of temperament. He was the one who really went in for nightmares (and my God, didn't he have them!). Mother would attribute them to something he had eaten before going to sleep (this would have been bread and butter spread over with demerara sugar, and two combination biscuits). Without having to be a psychologist, one can now see that they were more probably evidence of an over-active and over-stimulated mind. Father would provide the stimulation, with his own excitable interest in things. He did not set out to stimulate us; he could not help it, it was his natural state. Indeed, if the truth were known he would have probably preferred more placidity from his later offspring, to steady the keel at Fernley.

Although it is generally imprudent to claim, in the light of later events, to have noticed early differences in a child, it would be equally silly to deny having noticed any. They were there; and Stan was, possibly in spite of himself, early on his particular track. Only a few strokes of luck were needed to do the rest. The fact that he never left home to go to school was, in my view, his good fortune. Father managed to encourage his bent without at that time showing any apparent interest in his development: he might have had far less freedom under the guidance of well-meaning headmasters trying to "bring him along".

Cookham made no special claims for its beauty. At home, much as we loved it, we linked it with Bray, Bisham and Hurley. They were all within walking distance, and nothing of any significance ever seemed likely to disturb their peace.

Occasionally on our walks with Annie we came on Mr. Hatch or Cuppy Ayres spreading straw across the road in front of a house, and from Annie we were given our first warning of the death this sometimes foretold. In those times, people had their illnesses and died at home—sometimes frighteningly, as when a lad in the village died of diphtheria. Funerals were much more an affair of the whole village; blinds in all the houses were drawn down. Stan and I, standing at the front gate to get a sight of the hearse and cabs slowly wending their way across the moor, would be called indoors by Annie and would have to content ourselves with seeing what we could between the cracks in the venetian blinds.

But while straw was laid down to deaden for the gravely ill the sound of the passing traffic when it was almost entirely restricted to Parsons' carriage and Mr. Hatch's farm carts, nothing could deaden the noise of the future. The motor-car was beginning to make its appearance. People began to ride about in enormously ornate vehicles amidst clouds of dust, protecting themselves with goggles and veils. The early automobiles had much charm, with their twisted and highly polished brass work, their splendid coachwork, and a general air of being not distantly related to some of the caravans at the Fair on Cookham Moor. Their speed was modest, but in spite of this, on one occasion a car driven by an Italian incurred my brother Will's displeasure. He warned the driver: "I have young brothers, you know."

One or two of the more daring villagers went in for motor-bicycles, from which they parted company from time to time. There were skids and squealing brakes, and in the general mêlée a horse would bolt, and as it streaked through the village its anxious rider, dangling a loose rein, would be vainly beseeching: "Catch hold, someone", and the horse would finally stall at Widbrook Gate, throwing the rider who would fortunately land on the soft grass of the common.

On the whole we were prepared to accept these signs of progress. We felt that these daring people were blazing some sort of trail, and no one was more ready to champion than Father, who constantly warned against what he called hardening of the arteries. However, he himself continued to stick to his lady's bicycle, at the same time being more insistent on keeping one's eye open for the "*other* fool".

One day, while we were at dinner, we became conscious of an odd sound which we could neither recognise nor locate. The noise rapidly increased, and with it our apprehension—it seemed to be coming from everywhere, and was now quite deafening. Situations of this sort gave my Father opportunities to demonstrate his sense of drama. With his knife and fork poised above his plate and looking intently over the top of his glasses, suddenly amidst the din he flung the knife and fork down, and as Mother cried "Oh, William!" he ran from the room. We all followed him, exclaiming as we went: "It's a flying machine!" The village was agog with excitement, Father almost assuming the perilous role of the airman above—Henry Latham (as we later learned) at the controls of his "Antionette II". As he crossed the village he waved to us.

If we were lonely at all, and I don't think we ever were, for we were happily self-contained at home, it would have been when my sister Annie came to the end of her tether and the school beneath the walnut tree came to an end. With this our contact with the eccentricities and accomplishments of the pupils also came to an end. It had been a cosy and easy entry for us into the school world. Our minds were never clouded with the fears of examinations. The very worst that could happen to us was to be sent up to Father, and I do not remember ever reaching his presence: he was, as I've said, really a threat, and for all of us the threat was enough.

We were occasionally invited to tea by one of the pupils. Lily Heal, whose father kept a draper's shop on the Parade at Bourne End, invited us, and we enjoyed the experience of having tea in the drawing-room upstairs above the shop. There were other invitations of the kind, and thus we discovered that all the shopkeepers had their drawing-rooms upstairs.

Sometimes there were visitors to tea at home. We were usually considered too young for such occasions, but when Winifred Cooper, my Father's pupil and a gold medallist at the Royal College of Music, came, we were allowed to go into the drawing-room to hear her perform her musical setting of "Who touches a hair of your grey head, Dies like a dog! March on! he said". This was an impressive moment.

My brother Horace was rather prone to moments of religious feeling. One such moment followed the sudden death of Will Lacey at Cookham Regatta. Annie whisked us home quickly, but not before Stan and I had caught sight of the stretcher on which the body, covered with a white sheet, was being carried. We were not unduly disturbed by this. But when we went to bed, Horace came into the nursery to ask us if we had said our prayers because "what had happened to Mr. Lacey might happen to any one of us". We were not at all impressed. But for Horace it was the forerunner of a "call" to the Church. As his talent had previously been in such different directions, conjuring in particular, it was a little surprising, but my Mother encouraged him, and seemed more deeply concerned about him now than about the rest of us. A photograph on the drawing-room mantelpiece of Horace seated, with a large Bible open in his lap, was always a reminder of this side of him. Later he visited the Vicar of St. Mary's at Maidenhead who, as the interview proceeded, invited my brother to recite the Lord's Prayer. He could not complete it, and had to finish with: "And so on". Anyway, he was to receive many other "calls" of many different kinds—"calls" that took him to Australia, India and Africa. He was totally different from the rest of us, and in the quiet of our home at Cookham he found little to his liking.

In village life the social balance was broadly divided between those who regarded themselves as benefactors and those who, willy-nilly, found themselves elected as beneficiaries. We, for some reason I never fathomed, regarded ourselves as having a foot in each camp. Occasionally, however, one of us attempted to join the benefactors. Horace did so once. With the school now empty, and with time on his hands, Horace conceived the idea of starting a boys' club and by this means putting the building to good use. Mother was both encouraged and encouraging. We on the other hand were apprehensive: we had been and still were subject to bullying by some of the village boys, which dissuaded us from joining Horace's club. We preferred to wait and see what happened. As we sat in the dining-room, the voices of the boys—boys who had frightened us so much out in the village—now echoed between The Nest and our house, to die away down the path to the old schoolroom. What form the entertainment took there we never knew as we never went in. We hoped, though, that by this gesture Horace might bring about an end to local feuds that had gone on for so long, and that we would be able to move freely about the village without fear of molestation. For a time all seemed to go quite well. But then the voices we could hear between the two houses began to grow surly, and rude comments were made as the boys passed the dining-room window. When a number of dangerous trip wires were laid about the garden, Father took his courage and our fate in both hands and closed the club, which did not improve our position in the village.

By 1907 the family was very largely dispersed. Father was not getting any better off: certificated teachers were now on the way in and Father, with all his qualities, was on the way out. But Stan and I were not conscious of this. With Annie we now formed the household. Percy came home every weekend, there were the unpredictable arrivals and departures of Horace, and there were also from time to time visits from Sydney and Florence. But for some time now, background rather than people was going to play the biggest part in our lives.

We were always very pleased when Percy returned; he took us on good walks, and we never got lost. He was a wonderful bird's-nester and seemed to know the likely spots by instinct. Furthermore, he used to bring us lardycakes from Brixton. He suffered tortures of homesickness for Cookham—I know this because later I was to share this homesickness with him, and it was only through him that I was able to make my escape back to Cookham and all that came my way afterwards.

But these weekend visits of his, in which Florence often

joined, were not occasioned only by homesickness. He was in fact keeping an eye on perils ahead for us. As Stan was now more "grown-up" than I was, he may have been a little more aware of the perils, and this may have prompted his enquiry of Percy as to what working in a builder's office was like. On being told he exclaimed: "Not for me." But our peculiar form of education might soon be going to place us in a very difficult position. Had we been asked what we would like to do for our living, I suspect we would both have replied: "Stay at home." We had up till now never applied our minds to any other possibility, and in the circumstances it was the only alternative to a very bleak outlook.

Although Father may have felt that his boys were not as other people's boys, and he often spoke to this effect, we in turn may have felt that he was not like other boys' fathers. We were now approaching our middle teens. For my part I was still quite happy to go on making "one long bathe of a summer's day", and to go on enjoying village life, of which we were now making more of a success. But with the end of the school in Sammy Sandall's garden, something in the nature of a crisis must have arisen. Other members of the family, after perhaps shaky beginnings, had gone on to success at the universities and elsewhere. But Stan and I were left in mid-air. Father roused himself to take some further interest in our education, but of a very limited kind. After breakfast he would now give us instruction in some general subjects. I can only remember dictation from what he was reading in the *Daily News*, through which we were able to learn about Mr. Bottomley's bucket shop frauds. With this, our homespun education came to an end.

But whatever the inadequacies of our education, we owed a considerable debt to Father. He galvanised us by his attitude to life. With him, there could be no excuse for idleness. The stimulation was not artificial, though it seemed unintentional. And what could stimulate us was catholic in the extreme. It was not only music, poetry, and other intellectual pursuits that mattered. Father lived his life whole, and we too if we wished could follow his example out in the "world"—which for us and for him was still Cookham. Sometimes this wholeness for living led Father into situations which, no matter how strongly he may have felt about them, caused some anxiety at home. It may have been his odd excitability and lack of control that bred in us a hatred of scenes. We would enjoy arguments, in spite of Father's way of rounding them off with "But I know I'm right"; but that was different.

How Stan was faring inwardly it is difficult to judge; outwardly he seemed to be happily sharing our lives. To say that he and I were inseparable would no longer be true, but the form of separation now developing was too subtle for us to be conscious of it at that time. And something of this must have been realised by our parents, for whenever there was talk about what was to be done now that Annie no longer taught us, the emphasis was no longer on "us" but rather on "me". He was not secretive—the very reverse, and he was the least moody member of the family—but his instinct for isolation was already strong, and was leading him into paths that were his alone. Some kind of certainty seemed to have emerged about his future.

I was not literary, neither was I an intellectual. Music, for instance, was for me chiefly a matter of listening. Its impact was one of direct excitement. I loved the noise, and the sensations it aroused—but whenever I tried to give my attention to matters of musical construction and technique, the drums or the trumpets would immediately lead me astray. This could not be said of my brother, although he liked the drums and trumpets too. (Father used to say, "Beethoven loved the drums".) On the piano I had a rough-and-ready technique which enabled me to "get through" more pieces than he could, but when I was playing and he was near, quite often it would be, "Ah, no Gil!" and he would lean over and with one hand suggest a way of playing a phrase. I would not like to convey the impression that he was a perfectionist bore, he had too great a sense of humour to be that, but he was keen and eager, and these interventions were as much for himself as for me.

The most important changes in him at this time, however, were probably effected by his reading. His mind was becoming very active—really tough or toughening. I was content with Gray's Elegy, but he was discovering the Metaphysicals. It was his reading that was the beginning of our separation.

CHAPTER IV

PEOPLE COMING TO our door might very easily have been misled if they had happened to glance through the curtains of the dining-room window. The meal table was a place for discussion as well as eating, and arguments which might start in the atmosphere of a spring breeze, when fanned by differences of opinion would soon reach the proportions of a tornado. These arguments, which were generally above our heads and were mostly concerned with poetry, whirled around the room while Stan and I, next to Mother, got on with our meals. The exchanges between my brother Will and my Father would seem unending, but Father would finally give up the unequal struggle and retire to the lavatory, expostulating as he went: "My boy, I have given you my last word," while Will, now standing outside the bolted door, would be protesting: "But, Father, that is leaving it most unsatisfactory."

There was something of both tragedy and comedy in all this which, as we grew older, did not escape us. At one end of the passage, in the front room, would be my brother Stanley, drawing and painting, while at the other end, in the little bedroom, Will would be working at his Theme, the self-same Theme that he had been working on for so long, and which now seemed to us a cruel reminder that in this he was a spent force. Will was the victim, and Stan the beneficiary, of changing times. From the dining-room Will could be heard humming his theme over and over again. Gradually, as he came down the stairs, it would get louder, and if Father woke in time he would make for the door to get out before Will entered on his way to the piano. If he didn't succeed, they might almost collide, and then it would be torture for both of them, as Father returned to his chair.

WHAT MIGHT HAVE BEEN SEEN BY A VISITOR

We knew enough by now to appreciate that what he was composing was making no progress and he must have realised it too; so he countered it with his love of poetry. He kept thick notebooks in his pocket which he filled with notes about what he was reading, and he may have been drawing on these notes when he discussed poetry with Father at meal times. We felt a deep sympathy for him, almost an inherited one. We did not express it; to have done so could hardly have brought any relief to a man who must have gone through heavy sorrow and disappointment in his searchings for the musical equivalent of what Stan was soon pouring out in paint. It is sad to recall that what we wanted most from Will, if we could get him to play, were other people's compositions: I cannot remember anyone asking him to play one of his own—it was so long since he had completed one. But he once confessed to Percy that he was weary of performing other people's music.

He and Father received their pupils in frock coats. Will's pupils were more advanced than Father's. When he was not teaching he wrote and read: quite often he walked about reading. As a family we looked up to him as a great figure, and we never approached him in any other mood or ever conceived of replacing him in the hierarchy of family life. He was a dreamer. But he shared with the rest of the family a liking for extremes—in his case, for Shelley and the Football League (and in particular Howard Spencer, who played for Aston Villa). He was a great believer in mood, and he would prepare himself for long periods before he started to play. Sometimes the effort would fizzle out altogether and he would turn to Father on an entirely different tack, which exasperated us. But when he was practising for one of his recitals, which he gave sometimes at the Town Hall at Maidenhead and occasionally in London, it was different. Then there was much practice, and those who wished could sit round and listen to their heart's content. How different, though, all this was, compared with the conditions under which contemporary pianists prepare and rehearse.

The piano in the dining-room, the prize of Will's student

days, was showing some signs of wear. The dining-room being small, there was not a lot of space between the piano and the table. The piano was piled high with books and music, which occasionally cascaded down on to the keyboard. But with Will playing it, it was transformed. He was an expressionistic interpreter. In the opening bars of the Hammerklavier Sonata there are two moods within one idea and he was not afraid to mark this. But he put Natalie on to a stern course of Bach to correct too much temperament, and by all accounts his scholarship was impeccable.

The enriching experience of having Will so much in our lives made a deep impression. Looking up to Will in the way we did could have been an obstacle to our own advance, but it seems to have been a spur. When he played, we felt in the marrow of our bones that he was a great man. He went through his life unable to attain in music what Stan ultimately achieved in painting, but they shared together an unchanging sense of dedication. As he grew older, Stan was, I think, the best listener to music of us all. He also had the ability to play by ear passages that he had heard, which prompted Will to play some quite difficult Bach to him as a test; Will was surprised at how much he was able to play back for him.

In those days pianists usually showed their powers of interpretation in the works of several composers, instead of concentrating mainly on a single composer, which was more the practice later, and my brother Will's repertoire covered Bach, Beethoven, Brahms, Schumann and Chopin, though I don't recall that he played Mozart much.

In his own playing Stan concerned himself mainly with Bach, which he played very thoughtfully—and very slowly indeed. Horace, the conjuror, shared his gift of playing by ear, and gave renderings of Chopin in the overheated and at times over-crowded dining-room. There seemed nothing artificial about all this, it was just a part of our lives.

As was, say, Father's dramatic returns from his teaching in the evenings: he would get himself mixed up in the curtains in the hall, catch his head on the seldom-lighted hall lamp, and give a muffled and irritable "Yes, my dear" to my mother's unfailing enquiry: "Is that you, William?" It was almost a routine to forget to light the hall lamp.

My brother Sydney's position in the family is less easy to place. He was older than Stan and myself by three years. Large families usually gang up in age groups, and with ours it was Will and Harold, Annie and Florence, Percy and Horace, and Stan and I; thus he was in that sense odd man out, but was far from being so in any other respect. By nature he was far more studious than we were, and seemed to have benefited from our home schooling more than we did. He also studied under tutors at Maidenhead and made himself an efficient pianist and organist. In the light of his war record—he won the M.C. and was killed in action in 1918—it seems almost shameful that we should have regarded him as in some way "soft"; but the real reason for this was his kindness and consideration. When we wanted his undivided attention ourselves, in the nursery days, we would watch from the window for Sydney's emergence from school, and set up a hullabaloo if he did not come straight up to us.

He took his religion very seriously. After attending a revivalist meeting at Maidenhead, conducted by Quentin Ashley, a converted actor, he was himself converted. I must confess that Stan and I resented the change. Its real significance had little or no meaning for us: all we felt was that some change had taken place which put a curb on the overweening selfishness of our demands on him. With his music, his deepening interest in religion, and his reading, he was later able to fill a very important gap for Stan, who could not have found so suitable a companion elsewhere. Sydney was much in his life; sitting for him, playing to him, and in general making a good sparring partner. In particular, his talk about the mystics and his reading of Ecclesiastes meant much at a time of "void" about which Stan complained. Yet in his diary covering these two important years (1911-12) there are scarcely any references to Stan or those discussions; but this does not surprise me, for Stan was not of an analytical turn of mind—in this he was the very antithesis of Will.

In his lighter moods, Stan could be thoroughly appreciative of fun. He much enjoyed a little drawing I made which shows him down Ship Lane. He is saying: "What I mean about Rembrandt is . . ." and we are all listening attentively. A cottage window is flung open and the tousled head of Mrs. White is to be seen; she threatens us with vengeance from heaven for disturbing her Sunday afternoon siesta, while from inside the voice of her son urges her on with, "Go 'ed Mother!" Another drawing is of Stan and me at the new Free Library. We are sitting together, with a *Graphic* shared in our hands, and staring straight ahead with apprehensive grins. This is called, "Stan and Me Smiling to keep in with Bill". Bill was Will Allen, who was in charge of the hall and who occasionally warned us drastically of what would happen to us if we did not behave.

It was at the Library that we learnt the rudiments of chess. Armed with no more experience and knowledge than this, we found ourselves for some inexplicable reason selected to play for Cookham against Maidenhead. My recollection is that the match took place in the small Town Hall. When we got there we did not like the feeling of it, and soon after the game started there was an altercation between Stan and his opponent. Stan had thought that he saw a favourable opening for his Queen, and then changed his mind and removed his hand. "You've touched her! You must move her!" rapped out his opponent. "But I haven't moved her" Stan pleaded. But his plea was of no avail, and to a whine of disapproval from Stan, his Queen was snapped up by a mere pawn.

At about this time we became regular worshippers at the Wesleyan Chapel. I am quite sure that our secession from Cookham Church was not due to any theological differences; Father was upholding the Anglican Church in the organ loft at Hedsor, Will the Congregational Church at Cores End and Harold at Maidenhead. But as Mother was a Wesleyan Methodist, and had very strong family ties with Methodism, it seemed right that in her enforced absences Stan and I should go to chapel. Certainly the chapel services seemed to us to have more spontaneity and variety about them.

But one local preacher, a Mr. Frampton, came under the displeasure of the congregation, probably on account of the length and disjoined nature of his sermons; so much so that they asked the minister to remove him from the circuit. Mr. Frampton must have got wind of this. Harold, who knew nothing about it all, went to chapel one day with Lizzie, the nurse, and whispered to her, as Mr. Frampton passed on his way to the pulpit: "I don't like him". Mr. Frampton opened the sermon with the observation that there were "people in this building who do not like me". This created something of a sensation, and one member of the congregation called out: "Personal remarks should not be made from the pulpit." In the increasing commotion, Harold slipped away from Lizzie and ran home to Mother, shouting as he entered the house, "Ma, Ma! There's the wickedest man ever preaching at chapel this morning."

Harold seemed to have an odd knack for comments like this. When Percy had pneumonia, Father, who was going to Hedsor to practise, told Mother to send for him if the crisis arrived. It did, and Harold, sent hot foot, exclaimed as he entered the Church, "Pa, Christ's arrived."

Not all the services in chapel reached the same level of excitement and entertainment, and I confess to an occasional feeling of thankfulness when they were over. Sometimes the end was postponed indefinitely, for after the blessing and a decent pause, a general move to go would be checked by the preacher's enquiry as to whether some brother or sister would like to lead us in prayer. Sometimes I would cunningly shuffle my feet on the floor to set in motion a movement to go before this could happen. Stan may not have done so, but he shared my relief at getting out into the sunshine again. The sermons were at times long and rambling affairs, which occasionally tested us and more often the three little Smith boys sitting in the front pew; and as we prayed we would watch through our fingers Mr. Shepherd, in the next pew, slowly rising from his knees and at the appropriate moment giving each boy a thump in the back to bring them to order.

Occasionally, it was the turn of a Cookhamite to take the service. Then a prophet was not without honour, even in his own country. I cannot remember that any of the strange assortment of preachers influenced us very much, and as we grew older the services became more a matter of habit. But they could be interesting and full of character. When the preachers were impressive it was for several reasons—their personalities, their sermons, and sometimes their voices. One of them entertained us when reading the Lesson by varying his voice. For that of the Lord, he presented a deep bass voice, for that of the Angel, he produced a high falsetto.

On the whole we had the feeling that these services were by no means as bad as they might have been. This feeling was strengthened by Father's references to what he called the Ranters' Chapel at Cookham Dean. We never knew exactly what went on there, or where it was, but we imagined that when they were having their services they fairly rocked the surrounding countryside with their fervency. However, very soon we were to find ourselves in the midst of a revivalist campaign with all its attendant paraphernalia which usually either sickened or saved. We were neither sickened nor saved.

The arrival of the revivalist created sensations and difficulties in fair measure. He arrived in a caravan well bannered with slogans about eternity. In this he was hauled from village to village by loaned horses, rather on the posting principle. Arriving at Cookham, his caravan was pushed into the yard by the boat-house, and a local solicitor, who seldom took anything but an official view of his religious functions, told my Father with a twinkle that he had taken his turn between the shafts.

When the revivalist had settled himself in, all the miseries of his campaign were upon us. In the first place, the gentleman had, as of right, to be given hospitality on a high level, and when our turn came to have him, touches of the old grandeur at Fernley revived. Those in the village who were saved this imposition exhibited an irritating complacency towards those who were not. At the services there were repeated supplications from the altar to come and be "saved". There was no movement from our pew. Repeated invitation to "Come along, Brother" (or "Sister") did not leave us cold, but rather in a cold sweat lest our resistance should break down. We were not in favour of this kind of salvation; we mistrusted the whole set up. The black banner with the letters of gold, "Where will you spend eternity?" covering as it did our more homely and familiar one ("How amiable are thy tabernacles, Oh Lord of Hosts") we regarded as hysteria; and the "Glory Song", with Sydney at the American organ, beyond taking our breath away had little other effect. He sold books from the caravan, and when one purchaser afterwards wrote and told him that she did not regard it as suitable reading for her daughters, he wrote back telling her to seize it with tongs and cast it into the fire—but, as Father cynically observed, he did not refund the money. We were very glad when the revivalist departed: then we could settle down again to the more acceptable version of Christianity as we understood it—Low Church or Chapel, with at home what might seem an incompatible mixture of rationalism and mysticism, but one which worked quite well.

Devotional readings from the Bible seldom if ever took place. When Father did read it to us, the emphasis was on the beauty of the language. Most of his quotations pointed strongly towards mercy and forgiveness as the mainspring of his own faith. "Pluck thee the mote out of thine own eye", "He that is without sin . . ." He was very sympathetic to St. Peter. "Christ was a man", he often asserted. His respect for nature in all its changing moods made us believe in an earthly paradise.

We lived a kind of Bible life at home, as of habit rather than discipline. The experience gained in church and chapel was reinforced by our parents, whose philosophy and whose common language in bringing us up was the Christian ethic. Even if we did not read the Bible as intently as some, our standards were mapped by it.

But not everything about the Christian faith was acceptable to Father. For many years, as I have said, he had been writing poetry, much of it composed while cycling around the country on his journeys to his pupils. He was not free from vanity, and would often send his poems to the *Maidenhead Advertiser*. Over at Dunsden an old friend, the Rev. R. Hart Davis, who shared my Father's gifts and propensities in fair measure, was also writing poetry while visiting his parishioners, and getting the result published in the *Reading Mercury*. They vied with one another, in a drawn-out correspondence in which critical comparisons were not always absent, but there was nothing to suggest that any new ground would be broken by either of them. The verses from my Father's pen had been tranquil, as befitted a man who sometimes read "The Ancient Mariner" but more often Gray's "Elegy". So that when the storm did break, its impact was so much the greater.

The Bible-reading habit by which we were all brought up did not include the Prayer Book, and as we were chapel-goers this book did not come much into our lives. So Father's brooding discontent was able to go on smouldering unnoticed until it burst into flames, in a number of trenchant verses attacking the Athanasian Creed, which he published in the *Advertiser*. This brought him into the public eye and he became the centre of a storm, a situation which he always liked. There was talk of referring the matter to the Bishop, and it was even suggested that he might be fired from the organ loft. But he did not appear to be disturbed by the excitement, in fact he seemed to be enjoying it, continued writing more verses, and observed of the angry letters of protest that it was "better to be kicked than ignored".

A short while after this episode, which had given rise to some anxiety at home, Father decided to publish his collected verses, and in due course the *Advertiser* brought out a little booklet called *Verses, Grave and Gay* by W. Spencer. I believe it sold at two shillings a copy. A line which pleased Will described the gorse as possessing "fingers of fire and heart of gloom".

Anyone who imagined that Father was now attempting to make money out of his poetry would have been mistaken. Having made something in the neighbourhood of £10 by the sale of the little volume, he decided, poor though we were, to plough it all back into the cause of literature. As a first step, William Bailey hammered out on a copper plate the words "Cookham Free Library". With the money, Father purchased as many volumes of the Everyman edition as he could afford. Stan and I were despatched to the Post Office to get stamp edging, and for some time we were kept busy sticking tabs on the backs of the books and numbering them, while Father sat at the table with a large notebook in which he entered in his good round hand the titles and the numbers, and generally directed the new venture. Everything was now ready for the opening evening.

As the evening drew near, Mother voiced her only protest, that it would "bring mud into the house". She had no occasion to worry. The doors of the book case stood wide open, like arms extended in welcome. The shelves were weighed down with fine literature, and were impressively efficient too with all the labels Stan and I had licked and stuck on. Father sat at the table with the large notebook opened before him and a smaller one in which to enter the names of those who borrowed the books. Stan and I walked about the room, rehearsing in our minds the process of getting the required books off the shelves, and making ourselves generally important. But no one came. At first we attributed it to a natural and proper reticence, but as time wore on and still no one appeared, Father began to look at his watch and then over his spectacles. He thought now he heard someone coming. But no . . .

It would not be true to say that the venture was a complete failure, but was very near it. Now and again a book was borrowed. The plate remained on the gate long after the idea of a free library at Fernley had been overtaken by the more ambitious but not very much more successful venture of Colonel Ricardo, which arose out of very different circumstances.

Church schisms on matters of doctrine we could understand, and we could see that schisms could arise where dogma and rationalism were at loggerheads. But what happened at Cookham now was a schism amongst dissenters. But it was one that had nothing to do with things spiritual or theological; it all turned on a matter of bricks and mortar.

The chapel at Cookham was indeed a "simple Gothic structure for sheep gone astray". The balcony at one end was a harbour of refuge for the less attentive rebels, the press gang victims of compulsory attendance. Two rows of ginger-varnished pews divided by a single aisle leading to the pulpit were, with the addition of two lancet windows on the west wall, about all there was to the place. The population of Cookham Rise was increasing, but on the other hand the congregation at chapel was falling off considerably, and in these circumstances there was a proposal to build a new chapel up the Rise. That in itself would have been a blow to us ; I think we felt that our chapel was in Heaven already. We did not like Cookham Rise anyway; and there were other loyalties—one of the lancet windows was to the memory of my Uncle John Slack.

There was a meeting about the proposal, and judging by my mother's description of it, the force of prayer took a back seat. During the heated exchanges, Mr. Wigg was overcome and staggered out. ("And Mr. Wigg staggered out" became a catch phrase with us for moments of tension at home.) I think we would have joined the Buddhist persuasion rather than go up the Rise to chapel, and for for what we deemed our mother's sake, in an effort to save our own chapel, we increased our attendance. But in vain.

When the new chapel was completed, competition proved too strong, and in the end, with poor Fred Duckett and one or two others, Stan and I saw the key turned in the door of Cookham Chapel for the last time after the evening service. And with this, I think an important and significant influence in my brother's life came to an end.

It was left to Colonel Ricardo, one of the church wardens, to add the final chapter. When he heard that a fish-monger was proposing to buy the old chapel and convert it into a fish shop, he decided to purchase the building and endow it as a free library. This, he felt, would be more in keeping with its past: it should not become a place with a fishy reputation. Father liked that; he thought it very neat.

Stan and I did not go up to the Rise to chapel, neither did we become Buddhists; we just returned round the corner to Cookham Church. With our return to Cookham Church we were visited by the Vicar, the Rev. Dr. Batchelor. Apart from the enforced presence of the revivalist at dinner, there had been no other occasion when we were visited by the clergy.

It was true there had been encounters between my mother and the Rev. R. W. Rogers, Dr. Batchelor's predecessor, but these encounters, according to Mother, had been disconcerting. For instance, he referred to the Bishop as "the old buck", though quickly adding "But there, Mrs. Spencer, I do pray God keep a bridle on my tongue." On an occasion when he had asked Canon Nyren, of St. Luke's, Maidenhead, to preach at Cookham Church, he afterwards received a bill from him for the hiring of a cab to convey him home. Mr. Rogers expostulated: "What would Paul have said if, after he had sent Peter on a mission, Peter had turned round and said: 'Now then, Paul, fork out the money for the shoe leather.' " We were a little frightened of his appearance as he hobbled around the village. He had a glass eye which always seemed inflamed. He was crippled with corns. He carried a fish bag round with him, gathered stones in it, and on reaching the Fleet Bridge he would fling them all into the stream below. He left food on the doorsteps of the rich when he felt they needed humbling.

But the occasion of Dr. Batchelor's visit was to raise the subject of our being confirmed. His mission was a failure.

My father remained silent. I was only too happy to leave it to Stanley to deal with the situation, which he did so effectively, from our point of view, that the Vicar finally left protesting that he never argued with anyone before they were twenty-one. I don't think Father would have been prepared to agree, even in principle. What Dr. Batchelor had completely failed to realise was that in going to church we had only changed buildings, not Churches.

There was not much social visiting at Fernley. Our friends and neighbours seldom visited us indoors. We met in the village and as we grew older we relied chiefly on invitations to their homes. When we were young, it was Mrs. Rixon who took us for a drive to Maidenhead in her trap, strapped in at the back: seeing Cookham rushing away beneath our feet made us quite dizzy. This broke us in a little, so that when it came to Mrs. Wooster's turn to take us to Maidenhead by train, "to broaden us out" as she put it, we were able to take that in our stride. But a social occasion we did not like at all was when we acted as pages to Queen Elizabeth I (Mrs. Drummond) at a dance at the St. Ives Hotel in Maidenhead. We found the floor too slippery, and in a final mêlée we ended in a heap slithering into the fireplace.

As we grew older, we became more familiar with social invitations. There were occasions when Stan and I might find ourselves at a tea-party at Dorothy and Emily Wooster's with poor Will Aldridge, and others who shared in one degree or other his misfortune, but who mixed in village life with the rest of us. Ugliness, we found, can be transcended by love. On this basis some of my brother's later pictures—the "Beatitudes of Love"—are wholly acceptable to me.

One seasonal event in the village which found mixed favour with us was the regatta, which my brother recalled in his painting "Christ Preaching at Cookham Regatta". The regattas we knew were Edwardian, but our attitude towards them was Spencerian. The undisturbed routine of village life was more important to us, and these events were regarded as more of an intrusion than a pleasure. However, we joined in.

The village was a busy place on Regatta Day. The event was given a good send-off by the voice of Slender, a tow-path character, who was selling the official programmes. The village would be gay, with flower boxes in many of the windows, and flags and bunting, and people might be seen concealing fairy lights among the flowers and hanging out Chinese lanterns for the illuminations later on. The visitors would promenade in their fashionable clothes until, with the arrival of the band in their bright red uniforms, packed like sardines and almost buried beneath their instruments in a brake with a striped awning and drawn by a couple of horses, the Regatta could be said to have started.

The mornings were generally given over to the watermen's events which, lacking the social finesse of the afternoons, attracted few to the banks. After lunch the bandsmen began to play, and could be heard in the village, summoning the grandees to their punts and launches, and the others to the banks. The Regatta always emphasised class distinctions; there were those on the river and those on the bank. Those on the river collected themselves in groups, according to rank, and floated about together, holding on to one another's boats and punts, looking rather like gay little floating islands. An air of mystery was introduced when the ebony and heavily curtained gondola, with a graceful Italian at the oar, conveying the ageing Lady Radnor, came into sight. Sometimes the course had to be cleared to allow the passage through of the steamers, *La Marguerite* or *My Queen*: they were almost like phantoms as they slowly glided through the concourse of little boats to vanish again as they turned down the lock cut.

Officials now ran up and down the bank shouting through megaphones. The firing of a gun out of sight round the bend signalled that a race had started. Amid the din of a ship's bell and the voice of the T.C. steward clearing the course, it could be seen that otherwise good-neighbourly Cookhamites were engaged in a titanic struggle. If a close finish appeared likely, the anguish became almost unbearable. In our younger days the tension used to upset our insides, and Annie would have to make a dash for home with us. But most people took things a little more calmly than that. Respective styles of punting would be argued by the amateurs of the sport, in sharp contrast to the attitude of the watermen, whose sole aim was to get past the post first.

The racing over and the evening approaching, we would begin to feel more at ease. The illuminations would make their appearance on the banks and among trees along the river. Dragons floated out from beneath the over-hanging willows, and people clapped appreciatively as the river became more and more a scene of dancing reflections and decorated river craft of all kinds, with, as its climax, a procession of illuminated boats. After that the *hoi polloi* rowed about at random, whistling and singing the popular songs of the day; while my brother Will, who with others took part in a concert from the large horse-ferry punt tied up just below the bridge, vied with them for the attention of the highbrows. Looking down from the bridge we could just see him, surrounded by boats and punts full of people. The Regatta concluded with a firework display, which always suffered from a lack of funds, and thus did not last very long—a few bundles of rockets, some golden rain and Roman candles, followed by the set piece of the King and Queen and a "We thank you all, Goodnight", which was the official end of the Regatta.

The village, when we now returned to it, was a very pretty sight with its fairylights gleaming from among the ferns and flowers. Chinese lanterns above, seemingly floating in the night sky, were pushed out of windows at the ends of long bamboo rods, while here and there would be an attempt at a home-made set piece. There were many house parties, and in the cool summer evening the open windows gave the appearance of boxes in a theatre.

Of the Regatta little was left except the mad music and the glare from the fair on Cookham Moor, and on this everyone now descended. The gentry and their ladies in their evening clothes joined in with the *hoi polloi*: the "on the river" and the "on the bank" barriers were now down, and the mix-up was attractive and complete.

The curfew for all this gaiety was midnight, and Ted Keeley, the keeper of the commons, was there to see that it was observed. If his arrival was not at first noticed by us, the fair men seemed to be aware of it and to go crazy. All the stall keepers were now shouting the odds louder than ever. Coconuts were missed at a higher rate of missing. Anything that could go faster did so as the prices increased. As the clock struck twelve, the fair was plunged into darkness as though it had been blown out in one go—by Ted Keeley. In the darkness the crowds soon melted away, and Stan and I, returning home, stood by our open window for a while, watching as the last of the illuminations died down, restoring Cookham to itself and us to bed. And old Slender would count out his takings before he retired to his bed of old sacks in a shed along Roboro'. In the morning we awoke to the Cookham we loved, and he returned to the towpath to dangle his towline temptingly in the path of weary oarsmen pulling upstream.

This was the Regatta as we knew it. It was an outdoor social occasion in which, from our situation on the bank, we were able to take part almost anonymously, but it was never revived in this spirit after the 1914-18 war.

Different parts of the village had their different share in these seasonal events. The two sides of the moor, divided by the causeway, were reserved for football and cricket. In front of the Crown Inn the elder villagers played quoits. Cockmarsh was always the home of skating, and at times with its stalls, ice ships and bonfires, could have passed for a Dutch scene. No one ever thought of bathing anywhere but at Odney, and Bell Rope Meadow was the scene of the Regattas. And finally there was the charm of the Flower Shows, which gave us the opportunity to see the gardens of the big houses in which they took place. All these places came into their own in turn, and when they were out of season, far from being out of mind they became endowed

STAN AND I PUTTING UP THE NETS

with a kind of mystery, to be visited often as a respite from the crowded events elsewhere and about which our feelings varied as the day progressed.

At home we all found our niches about the house, so that we could go on doing the sort of things we wanted to do with the minimum of friction, and we all got along together with a high degree of success. But we kept a firm eye on Father's movements, and whenever he went out of the house there was a greater sense of freedom, particularly about the piano: when we heard him go out we would converge on it, and although we did not exactly fight for it we would sometimes try to push one another off the piano stool.

There would have been no favourable response from Father now had Stan or I revealed any strong trend towards music. He had had enough of this. When I played, his silence was occasionally broken by "Stop tinkling". Stan and I remembered with amusement the occasion when my brother Will was unable to play the organ at Cores End, and Mr. Blackwell, the steward, called to ask if Stan or I might take his place. Father adopted an expression of bland incredulity. Mr. Blackwell wasn't to know that the musical reputation of Fernley, however well established, did not extend to us. Stan's and my only experience of the organ was of blowing the bellows for Father at Hedsor. I recorded this experience in the form of a comic strip, which culminated with Father's retreating figure as all the stops are blown out.

We were now old enough to be able to understand better the general situation at home. That we were becoming poorer was self-evident. Father's income derived from the pupils was falling off. And with the exception of Will, Harold and Percy, "the boys" could still be said to be lying fallow. Father must have realised that the difficulties still ahead arose from our peculiarly personal form of education rather than any other cause. But the financial position had never worried us, not from the days when we had been allowed a ha'penny a week each and had early learnt the advantages of merging our resources in Mr. Buckham's shop, where we purchased scraps and transfers.

Really, money itself did not interest any of us, and Stan and I were the extreme consequences of a family tradition that placed most importance on things that no money could buy. If Fernley could have stamped its own coinage, the currency would have been poetry, music, astronomy and the like. But the house-keeping money was thirty shillings a week. I know something of this because for some time I cycled to Maidenhead each week to buy the groceries from the Home and Colonial Stores.

Mother was of course the one most affected by this, but she was a very proud woman and we inherited some of her pride, though with apparently little to back it up except the now almost legendary achievements of Will. The occasions when Mr. Wigg might have staggered out (and occasionally Father went out) need not be described. They were sad, and sometimes Stan and I had to take a steadying hand.

Over the years all interests were concentrated in the "danger zone" where the mind and imagination could be and were worked too hard. That it was so at times we knew; Will was a reminder. There were frustrations as well, and my sister Annie was not to be blamed for stamping her feet when I was born. But when an overwrought situation did arise, Mother would generally steer it back into calmer waters. With time and the increasing family, the earlier ambitious disciplines imposed by Father were relaxed, and the restraints in favour of mind over matter grew less. I don't remember any restrictions disturbing Stan's life or mine. For some time now, for instance, we had been joining in the football on the moor, and in other village recreations.

I was also drawn into another sport when Mr. Turk persuaded me to stroke a four. The impressive spectacle of the University crews training often drew crowds to the bridge to watch. Surprisingly enough, it was Stan who thought this new interest was taking too much of a hold on me and tried to dissuade me from going on with it—I never knew quite why. I did give it up, but not for his reason. Had anyone gone to the bridge to see us, we would not have revived memories of the University boats with their

HOW WE SHOT THE BRIDGE AT COOKHAM

beautiful rhythmic movement. The watchers would have seen us foul the bridge and in a state of complete disarray drift towards the weir, while one of the oarsmen was shouting at the top of his voice: "Get me to the land." It was then we discovered he could not swim.

There were two or three wits in the village who could always be relied upon to keep us amused with their spontaneous sallies, but the "suicide" of Pelham Fryer was more in the nature of a planned joke. He lived at Bourne End, and had to pay toll each day to get to his work at Cookham. Resenting the toll-keeper's refusal to let him through for nothing, he one day declared his determination to commit suicide, and with no more ado leapt over the parapet and disappeared in the water below. The ferryman gloomily advised the toll-keeper to send for the police and the drags. But all the time Pelham was safely perched on one of the girders beneath the bridge, out of sight. When he felt he had punished the anxious toll-keeper enough, he swam out and, regaining the bank, went home without paying.

Lord Astor was not prepared to throw himself over the parapet, but the fact that he had been noticed, one day, waiting for his ha'penny change was made great play with by my father, who found almost biblical significance in the correctness of His Lordship's attitude. This was typical of my father's way of picking upon incidents with which to point a moral. We sorted them out—and some of them we liked while others we dismissed.

Local wit was very mixed, and there was more than one claimant to the crown. Occasionally the jokes were more colourful than repeatable. Charlie Lacey was generally regarded as the titular head of a particular brand of dry and biting wit, and it never showed to better advantage than on the occasion of the Cookham Fishing Competition.

The event always took place about mid-way through November. Towards dusk we walked on to the bridge to see how things were going, to find Mr. Lacey already there. Through the rising mists and to the accompaniment of the plop! plop! of the dripping water from the overhanging trees, the fishermen, two in each punt, huddled closely to coke braziers, were scarcely visible. From the bridge Mr. Lacey, with a voice of almost caressing solicitude, called down: "Well, Fred, what sort of a day have you had?" From the now almost invisible Fred came the reply: "Haven't had a touch all day, Charlie." "Ah! well," observed Mr. Lacey, almost in passing: "Tis to be hoped that they will rise towards the cool of the evening." Fred's response was colourful in the extreme.

But there was one great event that we could not laugh about, and in which Father became involved. On one of his summer evening walks a villager found that the footpath in Terrys Lane leading to the Basewall pit had been obstructed, and reported the facts to the Parish Council. The ceremony of removing the obstruction was in the nature of a big occasion which brought the villagers, including Father, Stan and me, in great numbers to the spot. In all matters of this kind, Sir George Young, the Chairman of the Council, assumed an air of lofty detachment and wore a black frock coat. Chopper in hand, he broke down the obstruction and, followed by the Council, proceeded along the path to the top of the hill, where from our position we could see, silhouetted on the horizon, Mr. Parsons, the owner of the land, and the village policeman solemnly taking each of their names and addresses as they reached the top. Father was not a Parish Councillor, but this was more than his fighting spirit could stand, and slipping away from us he tailed on and got his name taken as well, and another anxiety was added at home.

At first the nature of the situation had not been fully understood. In due course it was discovered that the Parish Council had no statutory powers, and that these powers were vested in the Rural District Council. The significance of this information was not lost on us. If my father remained outwardly calm, we became inwardly frightened, and this condition was intensified by the arrival of a solicitor's clerk with a writ which he served on Father. He seemed to feel that Father was not showing sufficient concern, and as he

SIR GEORGE YOUNG BREAKING DOWN THE OBSTRUCTION TO THE FOOTPATH

left he observed, "This is a very serious matter, you know," to which Father replied with considerable irritation: "We shall see." Stan and I rather shared the clerk's view and wondered what was going to happen next. We were wedded to home and genuinely feared we might lose it. Our anxieties were not by any means eased by the complacency with which Mr. Parsons went about the village. But worse was to come when it was reported that Mr. Buckmaster had been briefed by Mr. Parsons, and further that an elaborate and costly model of the path and surrounding country had been made. In those days the name of Buckmaster was synonymous with an adverse verdict unless you got him first. Father continued calm and we got some slight relief when the District Council took over the case. But there was Buckmaster, and Father's position was still uncertain.

When the case came up, it must have been a disappointment to him that he was not called. But he had no special evidence to give, and had walked the path only from an inner conviction. There was one witness whose evidence it was vital to obtain. This witness, now an old man, was spending the evening of his life picking up coppers opening and shutting the gate on Widbrook Common. He declared that as a young man he had been employed as ploughman at Pound Farm, and persisted in his story that after ploughing up the land he had orders to tread out the path again. But he was obstinate and rejected every overture to leave his gate and attend the court, until a compromise was reached—that Stan and I looked after the gate while he was away, and gave him the money on his return.

The conversation at meal times had now undergone a drastic change. Will was in Germany, the poets suffered an eclipse, and we mainly discussed "the case". It opened before Mr. Justice Warrington, and Cookham became silent with expectancy. Father loved describing it: he gloated over it, and at times he gave the impression that he was the Judge himself. His pleasure when anything happened to discomfit Parsons was evident.

Old Willis gave his evidence. Later Mr. Buckmaster,

STAN AND I LOOK AFTER THE GATE AT WIDBROOK

rummaging below his desk, was seen to bring out an oil painting of a corn field—"the very field, my lud". Father would put his head on one side and almost coo as he repeated that. This picture belonged to Miss Heath, who lived in the cottage just by the stile and would not have minded seeing the end of the footpath. It had been painted from a position that was highly advantageous to the prosecution, and Mr. Buckmaster made full use of it. In the midst of his peroration—"this bewildering and damaging piece of evidence" —Mr. Justice Warrington asked for the picture to be taken up to him.

Now Father would echo the exquisitely polite voice of the Judge inviting Mr. Buckmaster to join him on the bench. "Mr. Buckmaster, I think" (and here he picked up his pencil) "if you look very closely and" (turning to Mr. Buckmaster with an encouraging look) "follow my pencil, you will see that there is a slight indication of a change of colour in the corn which closely follows the path as indicated on the map." Mr. Buckmaster returned to his place and tried to dismiss this piece of evidence now as not material, and embarked on a welter of imponderables. The case fell to pieces like a house of cards.

Returning home from Maidenhead, as I came along the Strand Meadows I could hear the bells of Cookham Church ringing. Breaking into a run as I entered the village, I found they were ringing because we had won the case. Stan and I had smartened up for the job at the gate, which was a great mistake, and Mr. Willis was not very pleased with what we had to give him.

Father, in his usual fairminded way, told us that we were to regard Mr. Parsons as though "nothing had happened". But something *had* happened and all of it to Mr. Parsons, and we felt it would have been more reasonable to wonder how Mr. Parsons might be feeling towards us.

CHAPTER V

AFTER THE FOOTPATH CASE we were thankful to get back to peace and security at home, and no one picked up the threads again more quickly than Father. After he had drawn the lamp towards him and placed his book on the table ready to be read later, I would carry out the after-supper ritual of fetching the cribbage board and cards for our evening rubber. He always played intently, and the score had to be confirmed by him before I advanced my matches—we always used matches—along the board.

"Fifteen two, fifteen four, and a pair are six, a flush of three, nine, and two for his knob"—"No, no, my boy—two for his heels, and one for his knob."

It was a nice game, not exciting but full of interest, and except for Horace's escapades, and an occasional game of whist, it was the only out-of-season game we played with cards. Bridge was out of the question: you could not talk and play bridge. Whether you could or could not, we all talked at whist "You revoked, my boy." "No, I didn't, Pa." "Yes, you did, my boy." Did I?" "Yes, my boy, you threw away a club"—and turning back the last trick, there it was. The trick now went to Father and the game proceeded.

Father's invariable remark after our game of cribbage was: "Now, my boy, bed!" Stan, who more often than not would be upstairs drawing or reading, would not be disturbed, and quite often I would be sound asleep before he would join me in the capacious double bed.

We had now been switched to the front bedroom, and my parents had taken over the nursery. This changed the scene for us, and the view out of the window was now perhaps more in my line, with my painted farms and carts.

Oveys Farm was just opposite, where cows deep in rich golden manure (the smell of which was said to be so beneficial to the health of the village—and we were certainly the chief beneficiaries) stood contentedly chewing their cud. Now we might be awakened by the cock—though often it could crow as many times as it liked without rousing us—or by Charlie, the milkman, with his, "Get over, Bluebell." But often it was still left to Father to do so.

On summer evenings we would look over into the yard, colourful with its freshly painted wagons, to the old red-tiled farmhouses on which pigeons and fantails kept losing and regaining their foothold on the steeply slanting roofs. Windows were often a kind of theatre for us—and the seats were cheap.

Another of my Father's abiding interests was in astronomy. He would frequently resort to a well-worn copy of *Ball's Starry Heavens*, and from time to time astonish, frighten or thrill us with the startling information to be found in it. Discovering patrons for his more promising children seemed to offer him no difficulties, but to find someone who would build an observatory must have tested him. Quite how big a hand he had in the project I cannot be sure, but I know that one day he took us over to Lord Boston's at The Wharf at Hedsor, and there on the lawn was a small observatory. Sliding back the roof, we looked through the telescope and saw the mountains on the moon.

Father's association with Lord Boston had not ended with the organ at Hedsor Church. They became close friends, and there is no doubt that they exchanged ideas and interests over a wide field together, and that this might explain Lord Boston's own love of astronomy, and the observatory on the lawn. Father was a devoted star-gazer; he would stand with his hands on his hips looking at the sky in wonderment. And he passed this sense of wonder on to us. He was interested enough in the sun and the moon, but it was the stars and their wonderful names that he loved so much. He gave lessons in astronomy, and Ruth and Lina Lowy (Mrs. Victor Gollancz and Mrs. Harold

Rubinstein) were his pupils, which invoked a certain amount of jealousy on Stan's and my part.

The great event in the starry heavens at this time was the return of Haley's Comet, exactly on time, just a little east of Cookham Bridge. We could not take our eyes from it; this little smudge in the sky became more and more dramatic to us as we thought of all that had happened in history since its last appearance. We were deeply impressed by it and we could not understand why other people were not so impressed. We were no longer reasoning beings when faced with anything of this sort; we could not take nature for granted, nor did Father—he positively accosted people, often total strangers, to point out the comet to them, and at times they appeared to regard Father as more of a phenomenon than the comet.

Also about this time, another phenomenon, of a politico-astronomical nature—Willett's Time, later to become the Daylight Saving Bill—captured Father's imagination. He threw himself body and soul into the campaign in its support. One morning on Cookham station he saw Ernest Gardner, who was the Conservative Member of Parliament for our constituency. Father was a staunch Gladstonian Liberal, and had been trying unsuccessfully to unseat Mr. Gardner almost since the Crimea. But he decided to swallow his pride and approached Mr. Gardner. Having introduced himself, Father then disclosed the nature of his business. Mr. Gardner paused a moment: "Now let me see," he said, "the sun goes round the earth once in twenty-four hours." With the utmost tact Father attempted to edge Mr. Gardner away from this notion, but unavailingly. Mr. Gardner persisted: "No, no! The sun goes round the earth. . . ." And with this conviction and a promise to support the Bill, he joined the train on his way to London and the House; but, as Father added with a twinkle, his speech in support of the Bill was not recorded in Hansard.

But while Father campaigned for Willett's Time, the ordinary sort of time was slipping by, especially for Stan and me. My parents finally solved my schooling problem by sending me to a co-educational school at Maidenhead. Stan was not sent, because he was now drawing so well that Father was seeking advice about his future. The drawings were a very odd assortment, but any artist of experience should have realised that they were greatly in advance, both in performance and imagination, of the usual work of boys of his age.

Armed with a number of drawings, Father visited A. J. Sullivan, the illustrator, who lived at Cookham Dean. He was a pen and ink illustrator, and probably at the back of Father's mind was the hope that Stan might be able to earn an income along these lines. But Mr. Sullivan did not think so, and Father returned discouraged.

Stan went on drawing, and I went on walking daily to and from Maidenhead. Will, who had by now settled in Germany at the Cologne Conservatoire, occasionally returned home for short spells, and when this happened some of his pupils returned to take short courses from him. Among them was Ernest Lomsden, the painter-etcher. On one of these visits, he came upon a drawing by Stan of a sack of potatoes and greatly admired it. With this encouragement Father decided to try again, and this time, perhaps with hopes of a patron in the back of his mind, he took some drawings over to Lady Boston at The Wharf. Lady Boston's enthusiasm was not excessive; if anything it was rather tentative. Stan was not "discovered". But she decided that he should go over to the Wharf, I think it was twice a week, to draw with her: she had been a student at the Slade at one time. Later she advanced him a further step by sending him to the Technical School at Maidenhead under Mr. Cole.

Stan was neither happy nor unhappy at the Technical School. His mood was one of serious application and concentration. My memory of the drawings he made then—heads from life, casts, and so on—is of the kind of work to be expected from a talented beginner: they were good and carefully observed. For a time, I think, there was a lull in his drawings "out of his head".

After a year at Maidenhead it was decided that he should become an artist and that he needed a more concentrated course of study. The Stanhope Forbes School in Cornwall was now considered. We had known of Stanhope Forbes through the Academy Annual in our drawing-room: to us he was a charming English landscape painter who would no doubt be kind and encouraging to Stan. But it would have meant leaving Cookham, and I doubt very much whether he would have stayed down there. Anyway, had Father taken those uncompromising drawings to show Stanhope Forbes, one wonders how he would have reacted.

The decision to try the Slade was Lady Boston's. Whatever effect the drawings might have had on Stanhope Forbes, when Father took them, with Stan, to Professors Brown and Tonks at the Slade, the result was immediate. My brother entered the Slade School in 1908. The sting was now taken out of Father's dramatic exits after breakfast with his "I hope to be home at half past nine"; Stan was also leaving each morning—still wearing an Eton collar—to catch the 8.50 train to London and, equally important for him, the 5.08 train home again in the evening.

To say that this was the turning point in his life would be misleading. It has seemed to me that the nature of his vision never changed essentially, though it grew more intense. But his entry into the Slade proved to be a most far-reaching and valuable decision—that is, if you believe in art schools, and in his case I certainly believe in this one.

However rooted it was in history and tradition, the age of the apprentice was over. The new direction was towards a greater measure of independence. To be trained and yet not guided or steered was going to be the problem for my brother, and, as I have indicated, there was an element in him, not of compromise, not of complacency, but of willingness. At the Slade this great danger in the period of training, which could disturb any young student, was avoided, since between the staff and the students there was compatibility. The Slade held a mirror in front of him, the like of which did not exist at home, and he saw himself among the forebears of his art in all their glory. It must have been a revelation to him, although in mood he had been prepared for this moment at home, in his experience of music and literature.

A new routine was now established at home. We would not infrequently take Mother's breakfast tray to her, after which we would leave home together, Stan to catch his train while I walked across the Strand Meadows to school; and, what was of equal importance for him and for me, we returned home to tea.

Afterwards he would go up to the front bedroom to read and draw. Already, too, he was beginning to perform his vanishing act, setting off to walk alone down Mill Lane to Cliveden. I would lightly discard my homework and, escaping from Father, would join the more tolerant Alice in the kitchen to continue my hobby.

Stan's occasional descriptions of his experiences at the Slade, and of the life, can perhaps be augmented by some of my own memories, as I succeeded him there.

He did not have much to say about his arrival there and his interview with Professor Brown. Waiting outside Brown's room could easily revive unhappy memories for those who had had their share of waiting to see their head-masters at other schools. And entering his room could deepen the feeling of utter gloom: the room sadly needed redecorating, the walls were bare, and there was nothing anywhere to suggest the glory of the place. Brown sat at the table, leaning back in his chair. Behind him stood Tonks and Steer, each with one arm on the mantelpiece. It all seemed so still and silent that they might have passed for a tableau in Madame Tussaud's. Brown would be wearing an ageing black frock coat with here and there some smudges of paint on it. Being interviewed by him was not an encouraging experience; one almost felt that he hated the sight of students. His face seemed flushed with anger, and it was only years later that I realised that he suffered from a distressing shyness.

A few mumbled words from him, and Stan found himself ascending the stairs to the Antique. The room was full of students and very quiet, as the masters Russell and Lees were going round. Later he received a visit from Tonks, who sat side-saddle on Stan's "donkey", his legs crossed and one knee cupped in his hands. His voice was modulated and he had an easy conversational way with him. He was tall with a slight stoop, and when standing up he kept his hands holding on to the lapels of his coat. His entry into a room was authoritative and commanding, and without side. He talked of dedication, the privilege of being an artist; that to do a bad drawing was like living with a lie; and he proceeded to implant these ideals into his students by a ruthless and withering criticism. His features gave the impression of severity and sadness.

It was always said that he was one of Professor Brown's discoveries at the Westminster School of Art, and that Brown persuaded Tonks to give up his post as house surgeon at one of the hospitals to come to the Slade with him as a member of his staff.

I can remember, too, Stan telling us what happened when he first entered the Life Room. It was "rest" when he entered, and the students were standing around smoking, and drinking tea out of marmalade jars supplied to them by Mrs. Cauffman at 1d. per cup. Nevinson came up to Stan, who told him that he came from Cookham. Nevinson then showed him a lot of marks on the floor, and explained that they were all that was left of a number of students, who had melted. If that had been the end of them, for another reason it was the end of Stanley Spencer. For the whole period of his Slade life he was never known as Spencer, but always as "Cookham".

Those were early days at the Slade, and the time had not yet come when we could chant: "I am the Lord thy God, thou shalt have no other Tonks but me." But a number of new names began to be bandied about at home, and Father could be sympathised with if he became a little confused by "Lord Have-a-smoke", "Tube Manager" and the "Man from Manchester", among other nicknames of students who have since become eminent artists.

The effect on Stan of his new life was not long in showing itself. His work at the Slade was orthodox: the ideal of draughtsmanship as enunciated by Tonks was based on Ingres. But Stan was learning only the words, not the sentences, which were going to be his own. In the realm of ideas he had early on formed his own way of thinking and of seeing things. At Fernley, too, the pattern was changing. For years the dominating influences on the family had been drawn from poetry and music. Now painters were beginning to make their appearance. They did not storm the citadel, neither did they get in by stealth; they arrived in Stan's pocket, between the paper covers of the little Gowans and Gray shilling editions of the Old Masters. And younger names were pouring in as well: Gertler, Nevinson, Lightfoot, Roberts, Rosenberg, Darsie Japp, Gwen Darwin, Dorothy Brett, Dora Carrington, Ruth Lowy, and many others. Somehow we contrived not to get them mixed up.

I can never hear a certain Chopin nocturne now, which Sydney was playing one evening, without being reminded of Stan's return to tell us of Lightfoot's suicide, and with an almost pre-Raphaelite attention to detail. His death was a great loss; he had been a leading light among the band of desperadoes who had dedicated themselves to their art at all costs, even if it did mean nothing more for dinner than dry egg sandwiches and Mrs. Cauffman's cups of tea. But in those days there were very few ways round, no side-lines to art. You signed the pledge in front of Tonks and prepared to meet your doom.

From Stan we soon began to hear about the monthly compositions, and about a most obscure body known as the Friday Club, the very inner circle of mystery. Membership was cloaked in secrecy, and I don't even know if Stan was ever a member or showed anything. It sounded as though the members took it in turn to criticise one another's work. The Club operated in one or other of the members' rooms round the Charlotte Street and Euston Road area. But the fact that they held their meetings in the evenings would have been a severe barrier to Stan's taking much part in it. He hated not getting home to tea, and still seemed perfectly happy to develop his ideas in the front bedroom at home.

His drawing and skill of hand had already gone markedly ahead, so that he was able to bring his ideas to a high degree of finish without the aid of models at an early date. Some examples of the sort of work he was now doing were "The Water-Lily Leaf", "Maternity", and "Feeding the Motherless Calf". There is little evidence in these of his new-found happiness with the Primitives, but they do show that he was moving away altogether from his early drawings. Two of these pictures—"Maternity" and "The Motherless Calf"—he took up to the Slade for the monthly composition. On the back of the "Maternity" he had written "Don't toutch" (*sic*).

I think he had been at the Slade about a year when one evening he told us that he had won the scholarship. There was no killing of the fatted calf, but it must have been an encouragement. Perhaps it was a good thing that the fatted calf was not killed, as only a few days later he returned to tell Father that "they" had now told him he could not have it. This was followed by the ominous postscript that his general education did not reach the required standard.

Later we learned that an angry Tonks then visited his wrath upon the Provost, and after a battle royal a compromise was reached. Stan was able to tell Father that he was going to sit for an examination at University College. Such news, it might have been thought, would have caused something of a flutter, if not consternation, but nothing of the kind happened, and I have no recollection of my father reviving dictation after breakfast or showing any other outward sign that a crisis had arisen. Stan, who, like me, had never seen an examination paper in his life, seemed to share Father's odd complacency. Still wearing an Eton collar and Norfolk jacket, in this state of happy innocence he proceeded to London as a lamb to the slaughter.

In the way in which he wanted to go he was becoming increasingly well informed. It may well be true that at the examination he said that Wycliffe had "instigated bibles into England" and that Madras was a watering place in the South of Italy. It would be understandable. On the other hand, he wrote a very interesting essay on Cookham, which I believe he also illustrated, and he was able, finally, to tell us he had got his scholarship.

It was perhaps not surprising that the Professor should have asked Stan to carry his bag for him on the way to Convocation, when Stan was to be presented for his scholarship. At a casual glance, his appearance courted such incidents. And if in his life at the Slade he came in for some bullying, his small size may have contributed to it. This aroused something akin to aggressiveness in his nature, as we had early been aware at home—there were many stories involving him in rough-and-tumbles. He could lose his temper: on one occasion he squirted a tube of paint down Nevinson's back, and on another, Nevinson had to admit defeat in a wrestling match. One evening Stan returned home late with a nose bleed, explained that "they" had left him upside down in a sack in the boiler house and "forgot". This had not troubled him as much as it might others, for he could stand on his head, a parlour trick of which he was very proud.

Although Stan was now away so much of the week, we could still go on leading our village life; and, if anything, more successfully than ever. We bathed summer and winter: Father thought we were mad. We boated. In winter we went sliding or skating at Cockmarsh, by day or by moonlight. We joined the cluster of boys under the trees at the top of the village, where they chattered and gambled away their marbles out of bags which they carried slung round their shoulders, until fading light sent us all home. When we were younger, we had been much bullied by a gang of thuggish Cookham Risers: in fact, there had been times when we were frightened to go out, and we would make a run for it to get home before they came out of school. But this jeering hostility was a thing of the past now.

At Fernley, we still went on happily in the same old way, rushing downstairs to converge on the piano whenever we

MARBLES AT THE TOP OF THE VILLAGE

heard Father go out, I still absorbed with my farms, Stan continuing to work upstairs. We were all happy according to our lights; Stan with his candle, me by the lamp with Alice in the kitchen, Father with his lamp drawn over to his side of the dining-room table.

The sound of a football out on Cookham Moor attracted us both. Football as played on the moor had more in common with the furious encounters of Elizabethan times, when villages fought desperately with villages, chasing the ball and one another over hedges and ditches, than with the stylistic spectacle of an Arsenal or Spurs of today. The game could be dangerous. All the manhood of the village between the ages of fourteen and fifty would be there. When sides were chosen, the "Master Spencers" were chosen last, with a hint of humour, by the respective captains. We were well pleased to be dispossessed of the ball as quickly as possible if it came our way, in a blizzard of hobnailed boots, barked shins and ill-assorted imprecations.

Our walks with Annie had long since ended, but in their place we now had our summer evening walks with Dorothy and Emily Wooster, mostly down Mill Lane and Cliveden. Mr. Wooster did not altogether approve: he liked going for walks round the village with them himself. (Incidentally, he was the only man I know who could burst out of a door that opened inwards.) If Enoch walked with God and was not, when Stan and I walked with Dorothy and Emily Mr. Wooster was. But though the Slade and his painting were winning Stan's allegiance, these friendships were very real and idealistic and meant a lot to us.

CHAPTER VI

IT WAS NOW that Stan produced the little painting called "John Donne arriving in Heaven". How this picture was received at the Slade, what Tonks thought of it or what the students thought of it, I don't recall; but I believe it never returned to Cookham, and after a monthly composition criticism it was bought by Gwen Darwin.

Stan once talked to me a little about the picture. One had been brought up with the notion that heaven was, if not all-enveloping, at least straight ahead. In this picture, he told me, he had the idea that heaven was to one side: walking along the road he turned his head and looked into Heaven, in this case a part of Widbrook Common.

Such concepts were a powerful stimulus to his imagination. There was nothing known to most of us from which this picture could have derived (though I think that the positions of some of the grave stones in Cookham churchyard were linked with the "Heavenly Host" in it). "Maternity" was the end of one stage for him, "John Donne" the beginning of another—and one that was to remain dominant in him, in different ways, for the rest of his life.

The room which now served as his "studio" was an oddly inappropriate one in which to paint such a picture. It had been our parents' bedroom until they exchanged with us for the nursery. As in the nursery, a fair amount of space was taken up by a large bed with a canopy. By the window was a dressing table which, with its muslin cover, competed with the lace curtains of the window. Between this and the bed he set his tripod easel, which may have been the one used for the blackboard in our school, and at its side there was an old card table on which were his Bible and the other books he was reading. A large, ugly chest of drawers, a kind of

Empire wash-stand with a marble top, adequately supplied with chinaware, and a couple of chairs, completed the furnishing, except for the pictures.

These included two long supplements from *Pear's Annual*, framed and hung up by Mother, in which oriental princes sat on marble steps at the edge of pools, surrounded by dusky ladies, and backed by slaves holding aloft fans of ostrich feathers. A reproduction of Rossetti's "Annunciation", a little Rubens "Descent", and a snow scene in which a lady well wrapped up in furs was feeding a fawn, shared the next wall with a text, "God is Love", picked out in wool in a pre-arranged system of holes through cardboard. Over the fireplace was the room's largest picture, of an old man with his spectacles well down his nose, who was intently studying a piece of paper, while on the table there were piles of bills and a reading lamp. Over his shoulder, and also intently studying the bills, was a stork. The picture was called "The Long Bill".

When I returned to Cookham after the war, and told Stan that I had been to Taranto, in the South of Italy, he asked me if I had noticed a reproduction of that little snow scene hanging up in the Mess there, and when I said that I had, his face lit up with pleasure, and he spoke of the cosiness of seeing it there.

"John Donne" was not his earliest painting. He had been at the Slade some time when he did it. Earlier he had taken himself off to the now empty schoolroom, where he had attempted to paint a Resurrection.

I can still remember it in broad outline. His experience of painting was then limited to what he was doing at the Slade —with, at home, a portrait of Father (disappeared) and a portrait of me (disappeared). This Resurrection was very dark in colour and tone, and simply handled, showing the central path leading up to the porch at Cookham Church. A number of naked figures had risen from their graves, and were in the air diagonally to and going in between the cypress trees each side of the path. It had not the conviction of "John Donne arriving in Heaven".

When I saw Stan in hospital, shortly before he died, I reminded him of this picture and asked him what had become of it. He wrote something down on a piece of paper, and turning it round I read: "I painted Apple Gathering on top of it." Looking at this picture in the Tate, I felt that its condition suggests that this is so; an X-ray might disclose an interesting "shadow".

When one thinks of the artistic struggles and the many failures of so many artists, the piles of canvases lying around face inwards, it is striking that there was nothing of this kind about my brother's career at this time. The pictures of his that are now extant are almost the *only* pictures he painted. After the first "Resurrection", which paradoxically he "buried", came the early drawings. The first was something to do with the awakening of day, and had in the forefront Mr. Hatch's old white horse with a child with outstretched arms being held on it. The "Water-lily Girl" and "Maternity" were followed by "The Beehive" (Dorothy and Emily Wooster), the little painting in which Guy Lacey is shown stripped to the waist with his arms resting on the hedge, in the same place by Carter's shed as in the later "Joachim among the Shepherds", "The Apple Gatherers", "The Nativity" (Slade prize), "Zacharias and Elizabeth", the Self Portrait, "The Resurrection of the Good and the Bad", "Mending Cowls", "The Centurian's Servant" ("The Bed Picture"), and "Swan Upping". I have placed these pictures in the order given in the catalogue of his Exhibition at the Tate, but I don't remember him signing or dating them at the time.

Every one of these works is a treasured possession in a private collection or is in a public gallery, and they had all been painted before he was twenty-four; and to make a fair assessment of his early maturity, some years should be subtracted to allow for our sheltered upbringing.

He read a lot for these pictures, he soaked himself in their stories, and he thought about them much on his walks. Father's habit of quotation and of reading aloud found a ready listener now. When I pushed old "Zacharias" around to get to the dressing table, it did not worry him. Nor did his twice life-size self-portrait gazing at me through the bed-rails worry me as Horace's hawk had done. It may be felt that our home-life was out of harmony with such remarkable pictures. Certainly it would have been difficult to have anticipated their sudden emergence. In some ways it was as though he had experienced a revelation. But it was a revelation to which his new experiences at the Slade, and the little Gowans and Gray books, and his love of home had all contributed.

He loved more and more his return to Cookham. On his walks about the village he would be peopling it with his thoughts and ideas. And the village was making its own strange contribution, in interaction. For instance, much of the mystery in these pictures comes from their strange use of barriers: the fences in the "Beehive" and again in the "Nativity", and in the drawing for "Joachim among the Shepherds". In the "Beehive" the fence is *there*: it is not a background to the two girls in front of it, but a curtaining off of the figure behind it.

On rare occasions he would include in a picture material that was not in the actual scene he had selected, sometimes for the design and sometimes for the sake of mood. But the liberties he would take were always small ones. For instance, in the "Beehive", the beehive was in actuality only just over the fence and round the corner from the position taken by the two girls.

For a possible clue to the mood of so many of the pictures of this period, I am reminded of those early walks with Annie in which so much was hidden or only half-glimpsed through fences or partly opened gates. But to attempt to separate intuition from vision in his case seems unprofitable.

We know that when he was occupied with an idea it was with him at all times, and he rejected or selected material as though he were out shopping. His nature may have had affinities with Blake's, but there was a strong streak of rationalism in him that would not carry him to the extremes which Blake could introduce into his everyday life. Stan

WILL PLAYING THE PIANO WITH STAN PAINTING
"APPLE GATHERERS" IN THE BACKGROUND

nursed his ideas and reared them among his books, on his walks and searchings, until his excitement, which was concealed from us by his outwardly natural manner, knew no bounds. Then his canvases received these ideas as though it was the end and not the beginning of his journey. They seemed to explode from the canvases. But at his side were the drawings which were the first fruits of his ideas: these he squared on to the canvas, faintly at first, and with light sepia washes brought them to life.

Having got to the point where he was ready to start the painting, he followed a precise method which appeared to be his own and was akin to the methods of fresco painting. He always started at the top. First he painted the sky and the landscape, then the buildings and any part of a man-made background, and left the figures till the last. But the chiaroscuro played a bigger part in these pictures then than later; and his colour was tonal. In spite of his method he was able to achieve this, finishing as he went. He was able to marry the Primitive method with that of the Renaissance. Only in the Angel in "Zacharias and Elizabeth" do I remember that he did any repainting.

Having started a painting he no longer seemed to mind carting it about the house. His most individual picture, "Apple Gatherers", he painted mostly on the corner table in the dining-room, before taking it to the apple loft in Ship Lane.

When he was painting in the dining-room, Will might be talking to Father, Horace practising card manipulation in front of the mirror, and Alice laying the table; he would just carry on. Had my mother told him, as she used to tell us children, to put his things away, I honestly believe he would have done so. But I must add that she never did.

When he did at times work in rooms in the village—at Wistaria and at the Old Ship Inn in Ship Lane—they were choices of love and not protests against home conditions. He never complained.

But in his solitary walks, and in his reading and drawing in the front bedroom, we respected his privacy and left him alone. It might almost have appeared at times that he was not so deeply concerned with painting, but this of course was not so. On occasion he would seem to look for others to share his experience with him. Dorothy and Emily Wooster often used to sit and watch him painting. The little disturbances that would arise in a large family in such close circumstances did not worry him; he would put down his brushes and with the rest of us carry out one or other of Mother's missions or requirements.

The drawings demonstrate better than words the sureness of his work, but painting and colour developed at the Slade by trial and error. I think there was some doubt about teaching colour, and life painting was not compulsory and was in the ratio of about two weeks for life painting to three months for life drawing, with an occasional portrait. I remember only one life painting done by him there, and he

FATHER READING: HORACE'S REFLECTION

did not reprove me for having only done two while at the Slade myself.

Steer's methods of teaching came to us as the voice of the Oracle and were the exact opposite of Tonks'. Steer was almost apologetic in giving advice, and we had to try to encourage him. On one occasion, after assurances from me that the chair was safe, he actually sat down. We profoundly admired his pictures and to be watched by Steer was marvellous. At this time colour was largely something you caught; you caught it unconsciously through the drawing—a kind of glorious measles. And there is something to be said for the argument that you can discover more about colour whilst drawing than by just sitting and looking at it.

But the Slade was, for me, still some distance away. I had now just left school. After two years I had returned home unabashed with nothing more of value in the bag than a certificate for shorthand. There was no reproof from my father ; his tolerance was perhaps carried to a fault. But I expected he realised that I had done my best to close a gap which in the circumstances it was impossible to do. I did not look in his direction, as he sat on the other side of the table reading, for any guidance as to "what next". But what I was to do next remained very uncertain. I still had no thought of following Stan as a painter. Anyway, Father found it difficult to take seriously the career of more than one of his children at a time, and now, in rotation, it was Stan's turn.

A first step in my career was in fact imminent, and although Father had nothing to do with it, it was characteristically odd. There were three shops in the village which one might call social centres as much as shopping centres. Two of them—Annie Slack's on the pavement and Pryce Jones the chemist (chymist!)—were centres of entertainment while the third, Fred Pym the shoemaker, was for religious guidance. Fred Pym, by the way, was our uncle, though we never thought of him as such, in spite of the fact that we knew his wife to be our Aunt Loo. She was bed-ridden, but sometimes she was raised from the bed and we would go into the little parlour and sit and talk to her, do her shopping, and generally try to make her feel that she was "all right really". Mr. Pym was very religious, and sometimes we would join him in fervency: we would sit amidst the smell of the hides, watching him dressing the leather, and suddenly he would raise his arms, hammer and all, above his head, exclaiming as he did so: "The King of Love my Shepherd is," and then, directed to us, "My boys, my boys". After these outbursts he would go back to his hammering, humming the hymn tune as he did so.

But it was Pryce Jones the chemist who opened up the promise of a career to me. He was a Welsh extrovert, who knew full well that if one wants to establish oneself in the world one has to strike out, to find a new approach and an original idea. He decided that the wheezy bronchial Cookhamites, victims of the low-lying Thames valley fogs, were a promising field, and very soon his shop was displaying notices promising a "lightning cough cure" with which to combat the coming winter. There was now much activity in the dispensing room at the back of the shop, and Mr. Pryce Jones suggested that I might try my hand at filling in the labels for the bottles. I had already had some experience of writing out labels, for the books for Father's library, and I had enjoyed it; Father always enjoyed printing and so did I. So I took the job, and all day I sat in the little room behind the shop. Customers were coming and going, the shop window was being cleared for the display of the cure, and during all this I could hear through the door Pryce Jones revealing disarming gifts of salesmanship. I worked very hard and by the evening my table was covered with completed labels. I stacked them in dozens and they made an impressive spectacle for Mr. Jones when he entered. At first he seemed pleased, but then his countenance changed. He wasn't angry, just very sorry. I had written on every label: "One tablespoonfool to be taken three times daily." At home what I had done was regarded as quite a joke, and the fact that I had done it at seventeen years of age did not appear to disturb anyone, least of all Father. Soon after,

Stan did a drawing of Mr. Pryce Jones which he gave him; it may have been to square him.

Many have wondered why, in the preparation of his pictures, Stan carried the drawing-in on the canvases to such a high degree of finish, only to lose it all when he started the painting. But this process was a part of the realisation, not of his idea—that he had already pinned down on the little drawings at his elbow—but of his sensations. He loved doing the drawing, he loved painting on top of the drawing, and he loved the pictures to their completion: there could not have been a dull moment anywhere; and this was so because he was able to preserve the drawing through into the painting, and at no time in this progress did the pictures seem less exciting than at any other time. His severity in "keeping the drawing", as he called it, was extreme at times.

I would not say he was not experimental. He did a woodcut of "Joachim". Pure fresco work was often in his mind; he came into close contact with Mrs. Sargent Florence and got much information from her. To get a result he wanted, he once crushed a green beer bottle and pressed the powder into a part of it. But I cannot recall that he was ever interested in water-colour. Occasionally he used them in his compositions, but for these as well he much preferred using oil paint direct on cartridge paper, without sizing it, so that there was always a fringe of oil seeping out round the edges of the painted part till all was finally closed up. It was almost like fresco in feeling—it used to soak in so.

The scenes or settings for his pictures remained a very important matter with him. I can remember, at the time I was painting down in Wistaria, that Stan came in and we went out into the little garden at the back. A piece of the dividing wall between this and St. George's Lodge garden had come down, and he showed me the view, rather in the way that we might have come on unexpected views through open gates when out with Annie. He did not say anything more, but the setting of "Zachariah and Elizabeth" strongly had the feeling of this view; he said, too, that he had drawn the Monkey Puzzle tree there from life, for this picture.

We liked least at home the view over the wall at the bottom of the garden towards Maidenhead, made sinister for us by the glare in the night sky from the town lights; and the gaunt shapes of the malt houses added to the sinister effect. The gap behind the wall was a dark trench of rusting and rotting relics of domestic life and, with the surrounding flint walls, made a very unlikely setting for most of his pictures. But he used it after the war for "The Betrayal".

His religious pictures at this time were biblical not only in subject but in time. The clothes his figures wore were of his own invention, but it is worth looking round the village to see if one can find any surreptitious borrowing. One of the figures in "The Visitation", said to be Dorothy Wooster, seems to me to have been disguised in a costume not unlike a riding habit, worn by a new arrival in the village. Peggy Hatch was true to life. And that strange cape worn by one of the figures in "Zachariah"—it could well have been a short fur cape fashionable then.

All these pictures came along quite happily. "Where's Stan?" "Upstairs, painting, I expect." He was much more upstairs than out-of-doors now. He would do a little landscape here and there, but at the end of the bed there was that almost twice life-size self-portrait. The painting of that portrait went on for a long time. Brushes wore out; then he would slip up to Mr. Buckham's to buy another, at about twopence a time. The handling was vigorous and the empasto heavy in spite of the fact that these brushes were very small and not so different from the brushes we had used as children. He sat to his work and only occasionally stepped away, contenting himself most of the time by leaning back or sometimes tilting his chair.

He seldom got into any kind of difficulty with a painting. His vision, excitement and method seemed a perfect trinity. But he had some trouble with the head of the angel in the "Zachariah" picture, and scraped it out several times before he was satisfied. He was very careful about faces. I think he had a mistrust of portraiture in composition —he felt that it disrupted design in some way, which may have been the explanation of his remark about Father in my painting of "The Crucifixion". But their detachment from human experiences did not make them in the least unearthly.

I can remember only one composition of that time which was objective, something seen and beautifully remembered, and that was "Feeding the Motherless Calf". All the others were creations of his imagination. Everything was assembled and put into its right position, probably while he was down Mill Lane which he once described as his "Holy Place", and all the canvases had to do was to receive them. In the whole of my experience I have never known anyone who was more ordered in his painting methods than he was.

He was now a splendid draughtsman—in the tradition of Leonardo rather than of Watteau. Ink self-portraits show his powers, and his insistence on drawing, during the whole of his life, is a rock on which he stood firm while building up his ideas. To me, later, he never seemed to thirst for colour as he did for drawing, though many of his pictures brought their own legacy of colour with them. He did not say much to me about this.

What he read, besides the Bible, was largely a closed book to me. But conversation with my brother, Sydney, was one means of glimpsing his mind. Another was to take a look at the old card table. Occupying most of the space was the old Bible, given to him by Mr. Hatch, often opened at Job. Struggling for space round its fringes would be Byron, Keats, Donne, *Urn Burial*, *The Brothers Karamazov* and *The Possessed*. He was heavily influenced by Dostoevski. Later, referring to those days, he regretted struggling so long with Carlyle's *French Revolution*.

He was unorthodox in the manner of his reading. During his whole life, I never knew him sit in a comfortable chair, for this or any other purpose. He was a hard-chair reader, and sat at a table more often than not, with his legs screwed round one another at the ankles; and a fumy oil lamp usually provided the light.

After the episode of the chemist shop, Father decided that I should "do something with my hands", and returning to his books left it to my brother Percy to make the necessary arrangements. Had it not been for him, I doubt if I should ever have reached the Slade. He had admirable qualities of seriousness and humour, to which was added some practical experience, as well as knowledge of what the problems might be. It must by now be apparent to the reader that my future had to be in one or other of the fine arts or in a blacking factory. Percy made a laudable attempt in the direction of architecture. He approached Herbert Bowden, a cousin by marriage, whose designs had been placed second and third for the new County Hall, and who put him in touch with an architect, a Mr. Wimpris. The result was not encouraging.

Undaunted, he entered me at the Camberwell School of Arts and Crafts, for wood carving, and this lasted a year. On the advice of the Principal, he transferred me to the School of Art Wood Carving at South Kensington. This lasted another year. I was living with Percy at Brixton during this period, until he realised that I was hopelessly homesick; then I returned to Cookham.

My brother Harold then made a very odd intervention. Knowing my love of farms, he found me employment on one. I was rigged out in a fruit farmer's outfit, breeches, gaiters, hob-nailed boots, cardigan and cap. It was Mr. Bryant's turn to dispense with my services after about two months.

After this there was a brief interlude during which I followed Stan's instructions to "get on with my drawing". He added that he did not see why I should not go to the Slade.

I was tempted but frightened. Looking over my shoulder, I took heart from Will and Harold: both composed, but one played the piano and fiddle and the other played the fiddle and piano. Armed with their example, and knowing that whatever Stan was doing, it bore no relation to what I was doing, I let him take my drawings to show to Tonks. I think Stan regarded it as a foregone conclusion; and with such an advocate I may have thought so too. Anyway, I was admitted.

Father's patron-hunting days were over, and it was left to Percy and Will, and to my sister Florence, to make the arrangements.

Once I was inside the Slade I had no more misgivings, and by the time I joined the Army in 1915 I had won the Life and Antique Prizes, Professor Brown's prize for four heads, and a consolation prize for the Summer composition, and I shared the prize the following year with T. T. Baxter. And, perhaps the most important "prize" of all, I was back at Cookham. The time had almost arrived for putting the middle leaf in the table again.

Stan's pictures were arousing a growing interest among informed art circles. Darsie Japp brought Henry Lamb down to Cookham and we walked and talked all day. The party included Percy, and as Percy did not feel himself to be an artist, Stan thought some special justification should be made to Henry for his inclusion. In doing so he paid his brother a warm tribute, saying that he seemed to have eyes in the back of his head and could find birds' nests without looking for them, and always knew how to avoid highways and long dull roads. Though it is questionable whether Stan noticed dullness. Once, on a walk, when we had passed through Skirmett, a village which was all on one side looking over marshy country on the other, Percy asked Stan what he thought of it. His reply was: "I didn't see it." That was the occasion when four of us, including Sydney, did a three-day walk, staying the first night at Great Missenden, the next night in a house at Long Crendon, and the third day we returned to Cookham. Percy encouraged us with rests and promises of bottles of ginger beer. During one of the rests Percy enquired the way of a labourer, who replied that after a matter of a couple of miles we would "come to an 'ill like that 'ere", holding his hand in the perpendicular position. Sydney lost the use of his legs temporarily. But we staggered home.

During the early friendship with Henry Lamb, he seemed to be always bringing or scouting for customers. It was through him that the Morrells and the Behrends joined the friends and customers at Fernley. Quite early on, Stan revealed an interest in the financial value of his pictures. But his method of replying to the enquiries of possible clients was unorthodox. To an enquiry from Mary Behrend, through Henry, as to what he wanted for a woodcut of "Joachim and the Shepherds", he wrote: "The price is a guinea unless they are poor or won't."

Henry sold my picture of "The Seven Ages of Man" to the Contemporary Art Society through Lady Ottoline Morrell for five times the price of the Slade prize for which I had painted it. When he had asked me to let him have it in London, I too seem to have lacked the correct salesman's approach. I replied: "I should be thankful to let my picture go again, even if it is only for a little while. I am fed up with it."

Most of the family had now left Cookham. We more or less shared the house with our parents and the pupils; and of course there was Annie. We found various "studios" around the village, mostly at a peppercorn rent from Mr. Hatch—Wistaria, the Old Ship Inn in Ship Lane, the barn at Oveys Farm, Lambert's stable, a shed in the gravel pit, our dining-room, the front and little bedrooms, and the school room.

There were more walks with Henry Lamb and Darsie Japp; a visit from Arthur and Hubert Valey, during which Arthur expressed admiration for some of the names on the graves in Bisham Churchyard; a week's visit to Gwen and Jacques Raverat; later a visit from Philip and Lady Ottoline Morrell. Lady Ottoline was not one who could pass unnoticed; she did not mean to be, but she carried the day most times and she carried it at Cookham. She and Philip fairly filled the drawing-room. Father was at his worst. Finding that Philip was, like himself, a Liberal, he introduced into our walk round the village a slight feeling of self-consciousness, of which we would have been more aware than others. Their departure was spectacular. The sight of a London taxi passing through the village was unusual, and especially with the two of them waving to us over the back as they disappeared round Ship Lane on their way back to London.

Shortly after this visit, Lady Ottoline invited my parents and Stan and me to dinner at Bedford Square and to a

STAN PAINTING "NATIVITY" IN THE BARN AT OVEYS FARM

performance of *The Marriage of Figaro*. With Father in tails and Mother in evening dress, we had a vision of the past. What we had not realised was that the Marchioness of Queensborough had lent her box for this occasion, and that no matter what, in those days you could not occupy a box clad in Norfolk jackets. Of course we had no tails, or anything like them, but fortunately for us Eddie Marsh, who had stayed with the Morrells the previous night, had left his behind. With this, and a suit of Philip's, we were banished to a capacious bedroom to change. To have to put on tails for the first time in our lives in such short order was a formidable task. But we found Millie, Lady Ottoline's devoted maid, awaiting us with the clothes spread out on the bed and a plentiful supply of safety pins. When she had finished we were all tucks, as Philip and Eddie Marsh were tall. The task would have daunted most, but not Millie. The trousers would keep invading and almost obliterating the shirt fronts, and the shirt sleeves were too long also; but with her mouth full of pins, Millie shortened sleeves, undid buttons, and added more tucks. It sufficed, and we got to Covent Garden without incident, though we did

WHAT MILLIE SAW WHEN SHE RETURNED

wish that Lady Ottoline had not chosen to walk there: the originality of her own appearance was on this occasion subject to some competition. But we heard *Figaro* together for the first time in a condition of extreme discomfort. It was, I believe, the last as well as the first time that Stan wore tails.

With all these portents, and no one could fail to read them as portents, life was changing. Much of what was now happening must have reminded Father of the early days with Will. The language was different, but to be bi-lingual in the arts did not trouble us.

Fernley meanwhile continued undisturbed in its traditional ways. Stan's pictures were hung in odd corners while "The Bengal Lancer", "Blind Man's Buff" and "The Sailor and his Lass" retained the place of honour. Indeed, nothing was ever altered. Father talked very little about pictures, because he knew little about them, but he could be proud of results. His way of popping into neighbours' houses—for instance, to play Beethoven's Funeral March on the death of Edward VII—took on a new form. Now he would go visiting to show a notice about Stan in a London paper or report some other triumph. All this affected him (justly) far more than it did Stan. I don't think fame affected Stan at all. He seemed to become more self-contained, though without any loss of feeling for village or family.

In London he was meeting more people. Through Sydney Carline he got to know the Carline family, who with the exception of George Carline, who was keeper of the Bank Field Museum, Halifax, were a family of artists. They were comparatively well-to-do, but Mr. Carline carried on his profession chiefly as a portrait painter as well. His painting of Mrs. Carline, disguised a little in a Greek dress, failed to get into the Royal Academy the first time. However, he painted the same picture again, and it was accepted the following year. (Sydney told us this little story by way of introduction.) A link between the Carlines and Cookham was forged when their two friends, James Wood and Richard Hartley, came to live at the Crown Hotel. They were art students from another world, the world of Tudor Hart.

Frankly, we suspected Tudor Hart's methods: we could not see what he was driving at, and his methods seemed to be the very antithesis of Tonks' ideas. But his pupils' residence at the Crown was a complete success, although we would give askance glances when "focus" and focal spot were mentioned. These principles were the keystone of Tudor Hart's training, and incidentally possessed something of Cezanne's approach. So far the Post-Impressionists had made no impression on Cookham, and how far they ever affected my brother, then or later, it is difficult to say. I was more affected because of my interest in landscape. I have sometimes wondered whether some of the happiness we were now enjoying may not have been indirectly due to them. We were evolutionists, and may have suspected the Impressionists of being revolutionaries, but the prevailing winds may have brought over with them a way of life for the artist, an integration of life, a new involvement; one thinks of old Camille Pissaro painting his pictures out in his garden with his wife and the children standing round, which very much accorded with the life and feeling at home.

Now painting in our various studios around the village, we would still break off for swimming, boating or football, and share in the excitement arising from the public spirited if misguided activities of Edward Cooper, the postmaster and grocer. He was one of the first to have a motor-cycle, with which he occasionally startled us. He devised a costly scheme for preventing the floods at Cookham—an unpopular scheme in other quarters as it more-or-less meant drowning Maidenhead. He was one of the first to use concrete for building houses, and fired by this success he now built a ladies' bathing pool down Odney. One misty morning Mr. Church, bailiff to the Goolden estate, hearing sounds coming from the direction of the new pool, picked his way through the mist to investigate. A figure emerged which he assumed to be one of the servants. He called out: "You are at it early this morning, George." "Yes, yes" came the

SIR GEORGE YOUNG SHIELDING HIS EYES IN CHURCH

reply, not from George but from Sir George Young. Axe high, he was repeating his strategy in the Footpath Case. Mr. Cooper had failed to realise that he was guilty of trespass, and the sledge hammer was Sir George's answer. He was a man of few words, and when later Colonel Ricardo gave a rood screen to the church, which involved the chipping of one of the arches, Sir George Young expressed his disapproval by for ever afterward carrying his top hat poised so as to cut off the screen from his line of vision as he proceeded along the south aisle to his pew.

Among the village excitements now was the sight of Bert Hinkler performing his "falling leaf" aerobatics in a plane over Cliveden Woods, with Monica Grenfell on board. Such intrepidity we admired, but strictly from a distance, and when Horace got hold of some kind of motor-car, it was to Fred Chalfont, the local garage proprietor, that the honour fell of teaching him to drive, with Horace going round School Lane on two wheels.

Father's pupils continued to fall off, but their loss was countered by a valuable local pension scheme, the Stephen Darby Pensions for Professional People. This enabled Father to enjoy a kind of Indian Summer. There were walks with him to Burnham Beeches, and to the Slade picnic where Brown batted and among the team were Gertler, Dora Carrington, Tube Manager and Lord Have-a-smoke—that was the nearest they ever got to Cookham.

Instead of Parsons, a bath-chair would now be waiting outside the front door for Mother, and she would visit her friends with Stan and me pushing—sometimes together, on the steep bits at Cores End or Wooburn, or turn and turn about when nearer home.

But there was an after-the-Regatta-was-over feeling in the air. Stan's walks alone were on the increase. In a diary kept by my brother Sydney, there is the following entry: "I went to church with Gil and Stan, the music was not bad, also Dr. Bachelor's sermon was better than they are wont to be. . . . Stan persists in thinking it is a most abominable institution because of its neutrality. After tea, we went to

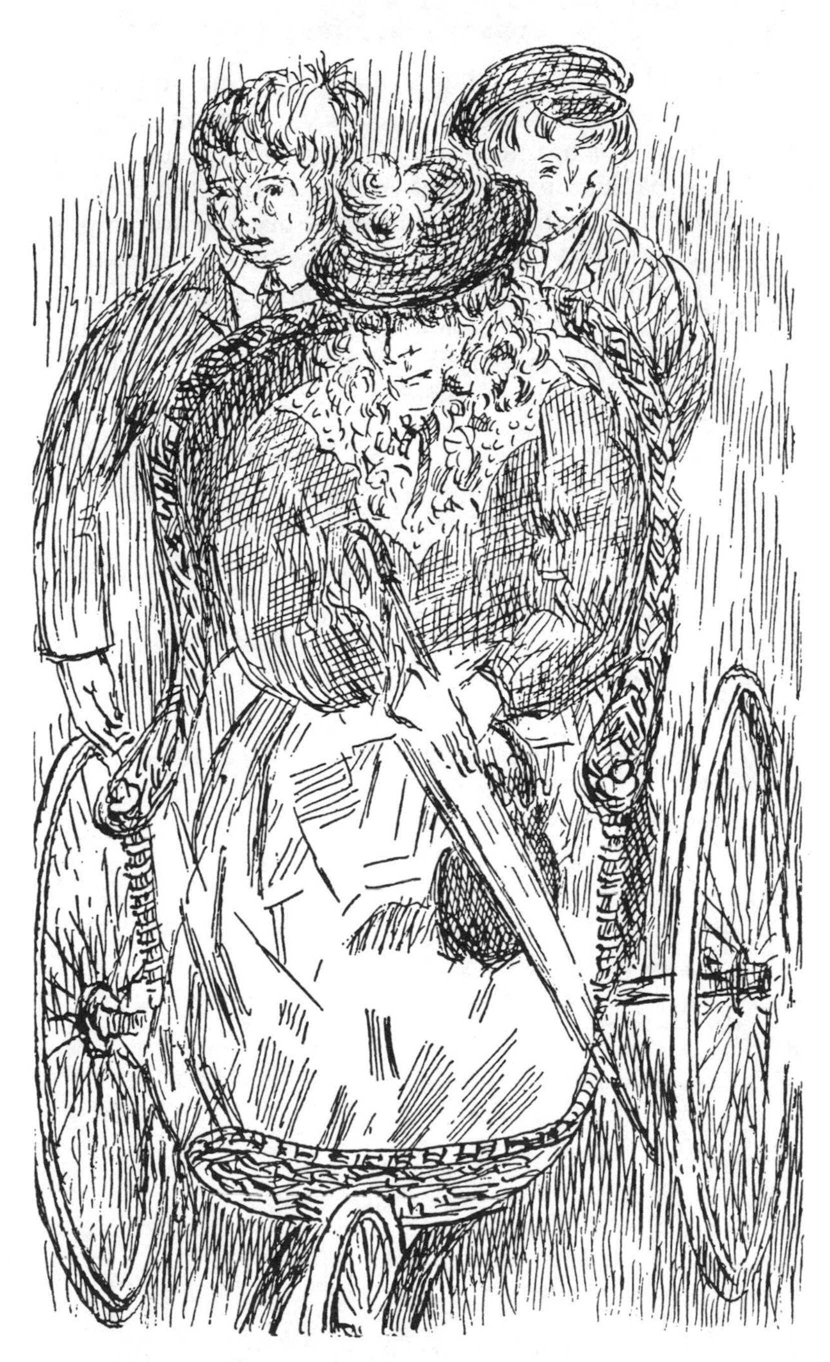

MOTHER GOES VISITING

church and I did not sing a word since my singing disturbs the equanimity of Gil and Stan. The parson preached a fair sermon which, under it all, seemed to insinuate nevertheless a hankering disbelief in the risen Lord." In that mood we were continuing to attend a place of worship.

A conversation overheard between Mr. Warren, the milkman, and Mr. Joe Bailey, opposite, in which the Agadir question was mentioned, did not affect our delight to hear from Will in Cologne that he would be taking his holiday with us towards the end of July.

CHAPTER VII

WHEN THE WAR came, we did not see it objectively. But Mother, if she did not see it objectively, saw it realistically enough when she declared that it was "no use the recruiting sergeant coming here as we all faint at the sight of blood". This she judged by the occasion of a family vaccination, when Dr. Plumb, waiting in the drawing-room while in turn, bare-armed, we proceeded from the dining-room, would receive each of us while in the act of reviving the previous victim, who would be doubled over with his head between his knees.

Rightly or wrongly, we had always assumed that wars were conducted by the regular soldiers. We had never applied ourselves to the moral issues of this question. When, a matter of a year or two earlier, what had seemed like the whole of the British Army, with General French at its head, had passed through the village, we had enjoyed the spectacle objectively enough. But the army was entirely out of our sphere; soldiering was a profession—someone else's profession—and the sinister nature of war was something that we had not thought about at all.

But it was not long before we lost our fond illusions. We were shaken out of our false sense of security by the early calls for volunteers for home service. These raised a serious situation for us. We were not pacifists, and there were no other impediments in which we would have trusted. If we did not join the army in some capacity or other, we knew well enough what the reason would be.

If the reports from the front and the descriptions of the fighting, now pouring into Cookham, were intended to stimulate patriotism, they had no such effect on me. A miserable period began for me, of fears, doubts, and distressing inconsistencies of character when faced by a catastrophe of this kind. We had no doubts at all about the justice of our cause, which made things worse; and here now was Percy, at home on leave from the Gloucester Regiment. Sickening deceptions began to creep in. I stood a returned soldier a drink in the King's Arms, and suffered an unpleasant sensation afterwards; I felt that I was preferring the role of the hero-worshipper to that of the hero.

But Stan, I am sure, never thought in this way; apart from the occasions when we ran away from the Cookham Rise bullies, he was always fearless, though not foolhardy.

As yet, enlistment was voluntary. We still had free choice, and for the time being continued our lives at home. On a moonlight night in November we swam from Odney Weir up Gooldens Backwater to within sight of Cookham Bridge and back. Odd bursts of "doing your bit" did not appeal to us. A drunken K.O.Y.L.I. was now engaged to haul Mother's bath-chair on Father's instructions. Stan and I would still have to push behind, doing all the work, with Father walking proudly by our side. Such bogus patriotism brought us no satisfaction, whatever Father may have thought. Cookham, like everywhere else, was now burning with war fever. But, as is always so where there is a sharp cleavage of this sort, what had been before and what now lay ahead was bridged by nostalgic memories, and for a time we continued to lead a kind of mirage existence.

My brother Will's holiday from Germany was over, but he could not return. The strain upon him of being separated from his wife, and of the uncertainty of everything, began to arouse fears of another breakdown. With Kitchener's finger pointing at everyone, he now seemed to feel it was pointing at him. He kept himself going on milk, filling his days by playing the piano and reading poetry, and was fit for little more. Stan and I did all we could to reassure him, but he went into the village and consulted a strange apparition of a man, a Mr. Haig, who, on account of his name and his way of dressing, we had nicknamed "The Hague Convention". This self-appointed recruiting sergeant invited people to consult him, if they so desired, before responding to a banner that was spread across the front of the butcher's shop, calling upon them to join the "Sportsman's Battalion".

At home now we were warlike in our unpreparedness for war. One could not ask Will to pass the bread knife without a dissertation on its significance. Fortunately he was soon given permission to go to Switzerland, where his wife was allowed to join him; a happy interlude in the progress of misery. He was most kindly received there, and when finally he died at Thün, the speaker at his funeral declared that "Herr Spencer came to Switzerland a great Englishman and died a great Swiss".

By Christmas the retreat on the Western Front was halted and our troops had dug in. Although we did not realise it at the time, this was the end of any hopes of a short war, and not until the emergence of the tanks was there any hint of how the impasse of trench warfare might be ended.

For a while Stan continued to paint "Swan Upping" and I continued to go to the Slade. But it was all becoming unreal and seemingly futile, and I now know that Stan, who never opened out at home as to his feelings, was writing to Henry Lamb, asking him to try to get him into a "decent regiment", explaining that he would be much happier doing something different and that the only obstacle was Mother. All his fears seemed to be not of the danger but of the boredom. Boredom frightened him more than anything in the world, and he evaded it like the devil all his life.

If he was going into the war, there was only one stipulation that he made—that he should take with him some of his dearest friends: Giotto, Fra Angelico, Masaccio and Giorgione. Whatever effect the war was having on him, he could still write letters, exciting and vivid ones, entirely about the artists he was discovering in the Gowans and Gray books and about his own pictures: "Peter casting his Shadow over the Cripple", and another which was probably "Swan Upping" ("I am starting a masterpiece, I wish you could see it"). One thing is quite clear. In spite of the war and the fact that we were now rushing about Kidwells Park with wooden rifles under Sergeant-Major Baldwin, he could curtain that all off when he wanted to.

Cookham was fast losing its manpower, and we knew that sooner or later it would have to lose us if we were not going to lose our manhood as well. Stan and I had for some time been attending St. John's Ambulance lectures, given by a foreman ganger on the railway at Maidenhead, who used to stress the necessity for prompt action by describing how one of his men, who had severely damaged a knee, cried out as he fell: "Save my synovial oil"—from which we concluded that he too must have been a St. John's man.

I had no more reasons left for not joining something. Unlike Stan, I was miserable all the time, but of course I was at a very different stage as an artist than he was. He had had six years of the Slade and other excitements, whilst I had just completed about eighteen months as a part-timer, with a third of it under war conditions. In this mood I told Stan I was going to join the R.A.M.C., as I could not stand the thought of bayonet fighting—adding that I did not see why he should do anything.

So it came about that I found myself, with two or three villagers, *en route* for Bristol where we enlisted. Enlisting in those days was a very brief business, taking ten minutes or so at the outside, with a little extra time for pinning on our coats a cardboard Union Jack with "Citizens of Bristol" stamped over it. From the recruiting station we went by tram to the Beaufort War Hospital at Fishponds, which in peacetime was the County Asylum. Here and there, through gaps in the rhododendrons which bordered the drive, we could see well-kept lawns and flower-beds, while away in the distance a knot of what appeared to be very tall men, all in black and wearing flattish black felt hats, pushed and pulled a heavy roller over a cricket pitch, with a uniformed warder in charge of them. Round a corner we came in sight of the Asylum. Anything less likely to provoke creative art it would be impossible to imagine. I need not describe it: you have only to think of any asylum on the outskirts of any great city, down to the clock on the roof of the administration block, and there you have it.

As we had arrived about 4.30 I had thoughts of tea, our favourite meal at home. A sergeant-major and one or two warders came out of the administration block. At that time I was not very experienced in sergeant-majors, but this one was, I am sure, different from anything I could have imagined. He hardly seemed to know that he was a sergeant-major. He wore an expression of detachment almost amounting to boredom. His uniform was khaki in colour, but surely no sergeant-major ever took a parade in so misfitting a uniform as that, and his hat appeared by its own volition to be fast reverting to the kind worn by superintendents of asylums. After a brief perusal of us, he said "Right turn", almost in an undertone, and one of the warders marched us off crocodile-fashion in the direction of the wards. As we walked through them, one by one we peeled off to find ourselves "on duty".

With so phenomenally little experience, I felt useless and in the way. What was I to do? The ward was full of wounded Gallipoli soldiers, their skins sunburnt and their clothes bleached, and the soil of Suvla Bay still on their boots. The sister and doctors moved among them calmly and confidently, attended by a nursing orderly who knew exactly what he was doing. If any of them looked in my direction I tried to evade their glances; if I failed, I stood to attention. They were all too busy to attend to me, but I did hear the sister say to one of the nurses, "Is that the new orderly?", and by this I concluded that an overdue promise from the administration block had now been fulfilled.

After a period of trying to walk up and down the ward purposefully with no purpose at all, I was sent by George, the nursing orderly, to "see Sister". The interview was brief. She told me I must be very clean, and after one or two further comments she handed me back to George. Following him down the ward, we came to a series of lavatories, one of which had been set apart and was full of what, in another form, my mother used to refer to as "certain articles". That was my baptism of fire. It is, of course, the text-book routine for beginners in nursing.

When Stan and I had joined the St. John's Ambulance Brigade, it was not as part of any plan, but rather as a way of filling in the period of indecision. So when Stan joined me at Bristol in June 1915, it was because I had gone there; had I gone elsewhere, no matter where or what I had joined, he would have joined me, as he did now, wearing his straw boater and carrying a little Gladstone-bag.

Everything that had meant so much to him at Cookham, if it had not quite vanished, was now in abeyance. The war had already reduced us to what might almost be called a blessed state of servility, making it possible for us, as for most people, to accept our changed circumstances and to perform so many menial and dull tasks without finding them intolerable. Tonks, one feels, would almost have accepted a bad drawing as a good one, in wartime.

I was not consciously aware of this at the time, and Stan's allegation that when he first caught sight of me through the glass partition, on his arrival in Ward A, I was prancing down the ward astride my broom, may well have been true. But what I am attempting to understand now is the plight of my brother, as I often saw *him* through the partition, carrying out the routine tasks of an orderly, which were so remote from all that he had been achieving at Cookham.

Letters of his to Henry Lamb show that he was keenly aware of how incongruous the switch was, but even in these letters his excitement in recording everything was vivid. Which goes to show that these experiences too played an essential part in his process of finding his way into the heart of his ideas. But to all intents and purposes he was now, for a time, nothing more than the orderly in Ward A. Occasionally we worked together on dressings, and it was not long before we became tolerably useful.

But how he cursed having to scrub the bathroom—a misleading term, as the room contained six baths, about twenty hand basins, and a huge acreage of floor. I once tried to deceive the sister by using a mop instead of a scrubbing brush, but was caught and made to do the job again. Later she observed: "There are no corners to Spencer's Ward."

As we got to know more about the hospital, we realised that it had been more dangerous there in peacetime than during the war. The knives and forks seemed to have been constructed more for the protection of life and limb than for eating: all were blunted down to the minimum. The plates and dishes were made of tin, and when the feeble-minded George cleared away, he laid his arm across the top of the table and swept the whole lot off at the other end into a large basket.

Beyond the satisfaction of doing something definitely connected with the war, there were no other compensations. There was no social life outside the hospital at all. There seemed to be no one at Bristol who would know that Stan was there. For some time he continued in his anonymous position as the orderly of Ward A and rubbed along with the rest of us, chanting the Death of Poor Cock Robin in front of the administrative block, or joining in with us in an effort to express our disapproval of Bugler Willett, who disturbed our mornings, in a stanza which ran thus:

There it goes,
Who knows
Who blows?
Out of his billet
Stepped little Willett,
He knows
Who blew it.

But in Henry Lamb he seemed to find an outlet for all his pent-up feelings. "If only I could get exercise or drilling—I know all about drilling—in some infantry regiment, Bantams or something. I see they are asking for volunteers for foreign service."

My feelings were pent-up too, though not for the same

reasons. I resolved them by transferring to Aldershot, to go overseas. This prompted a postcard to Henry in which Stan expressed his feelings on my departure in such simple sorrowing terms that, had I seen it at the time, I would not have dreamt of leaving Bristol.

His repeated references at this time to his choice of an infantry regiment—"Bantams or something"—are an indication that he was sensitive about his size. But there was no need for this. He did not convey the impression of being dwarfish, although it must be said that when he got his uniform there was something of a recurrence of the difficulties we had encountered when we dressed for *Figaro*.

How he balanced his life at Bristol after I left I never knew, but that he was becoming increasingly unhappy there one gathers from his letters to Henry. But his social life at Bristol picked up quite a bit when it became more known who he was. He started drawing heads again. The Desmond Chutes got wind of his presence and he spent many happy hours at their house listening to Desmond playing early English music. One or two of the doctors at the hospital took him up as well. But the death of an orderly of whom he was very fond upset him greatly. The orderly had said how awful it would be to die there, and Stan had felt the same, and now the orderly had died.

He left Bristol early in 1916, and we "dipped flags" to one another as our ships passed in the Mediterranean. From Salonika, which was his destination, he could write again to Henry Lamb that he was sitting on some rocks up the line, carving heads out of some soft stone with a knife; and again, "I have got a fine lot of books, it would repay you to come over on your charger" (Henry had a horse) "and see them". He "felt quite rich now", and sent £5 to our parents, adding that he was sure they were all right now as all the Spencers were in the Army and quite rich.

I had sent a note to my bank to transfer my assets (which would have been the money Henry had collected for me by selling my "Seven Ages" picture and one or two others) to Father. But I cannot confirm my brother's view that we were rich. In Cairo, three months on infantry pay did not get one far; but I did get to the Pyramids for ten piastres with a padre's party.

Through Henry we know something of my brother's reading at this time. In three months, he declared, he had read all Shakespeare's historical plays, *Edward II* and *The Jew of Malta*, *Paradise Lost*, and four of Shakespeare's comedies, as well as occasionally dissipating himself on such "wasteful destructive stuff" as *Lavengro*. Keats and Blake he read together. He thought Blake was a great poet, who made him long for Marvell and Donatello. He thought Claude a very great artist; he could not understand how Turner could aspire to have his name coupled with Claude's and regarded it as blasphemy to imagine Claude painting "Wind, Rain and Steam".

He was enquiring of Henry if he were not aching for Gluck, Mozart, Bach and Beethoven. Here, then, was detachment of mind coming out of the trenches in Salonika in 1917. This was my brother at twenty-six while I at twenty-five on the Sinai Desert read the *Iliad* but was much happier with *Pickwick Papers*.

I did one of the best drawings then that I have ever done, of one of the sisters, and very nearly repeated my success with another sister. But she did not like her drawing and I found it rubbed out. I was very hurt by this, and was further damped by the arrival of James McBey as the official war artist. I was not introduced to him: he did not know I was there, but it was very much brought home to me that he was.

Let me here interpose, for the record, a brief account of my war experiences, and be done with it. After leaving Bristol, on draft for Middle East, picked out for padre's batman. Never saw padre. Arrived Salonika November 1915. Found we were 28 General Hospital, pitched Hospital at Dudula. Officers' servant. Involved in dump fire. Discovered Olympus in remarkable circumstances. At the time had no idea of its name, but as it looked fairly close, thought I would walk over and have a look at it.

THE DUMP-FIRE AT SALONIKA

Officer stopped me, told me it was sixty miles away, and added: "And that mountain happens to be Olympus."

Designed menu card for Christmas dinner officers' mess, spelt "tomato" with an "r" and peas the wrong way in Green Peas. Bombed several times, noted my conduct was same as everyone else's. Heard Darsie Japp was commanding battery up the line. Asked for transfer to artillery. Found myself on board s.s. *Letitia*, five months at sea. Copied photo of corporal's wife, did fine drawing of three-master at Marseilles. Corporal said he preferred the ship, gave him both.

Went to England and to Cookham, very quiet and beautiful. Returned to Alexandria, asked to be put ashore, paraded at Sidi Gaba to join Stan in Salonika. Quoted the rule, found myself in the dysentery hut at 17 General Hospital. Stayed there a year, finest job I did during war. On draft 36 Stationary Hospital, Sinai Desert. Repeatedly had charge of ward alone, very proud of this. Lost eyebrows sterilising instruments on a primus stove. Volunteered for infantry, sent to Cairo—Zeitoun for training. Joined East Surreys (Hackney Gurkhas) at Kantara. Turks surrendered. Saw no fighting. Lost forty prisoners, found them again. Returned to England March 1919.

Stan returned to England in December 1918. He had been ill with malaria, and from the day he set foot in Salonika he had been up the line the whole time and was often in great danger. He told me that on one occasion he was out reconnoitring with his officer when they realised they were near a Bulgar machine-gun post. The officer, in spite of my brother's advice, fired on the post, and was badly wounded in return. Stan had to drag him to cover. When he returned home he told this story to Eddie Marsh, who asked, "Well Stanley, would you like an M.M.?" Stan mimicked Eddie's high voice to the life.

On another occasion he had mounted a horse because he was tired. The horse took him out into a river, and he could not get it to return. A Jock sergeant was sent to fetch him back and was so angry that he hit Stan. A soldier who had witnessed this incident, and disapproved, took my brother to one side and gave him some boxing lessons. He then went into the ring with his adversary; but, Stan added, "It was no good, I was bowled over straight away."

(Years later he was lodging over a rather high-brow bookshop which Henry Lamb called the "Betterment Bookshop". Stanley, meaning no harm, used the name to the lady who owned it, who promptly smacked him. I never came in for this sort of treatment, because my appearance suggested that I might prove less mild. Had people known, they were in far greater danger when they attacked him. He had a way of going wild, as Nevison had discovered at the Slade.)

We know that Stanley was in the final advance—in other words, that he went "over the top". It must have been a great satisfaction to him to have weathered such invaluable experiences. True, he lost a "whole book of drawings" on his way home, he told me, but that might mean anything; he would draw on anything. We know, however, that he went back to that particular sector for the setting of his "Resurrection of the Soldiers" at Burghclere: he must have been thinking a lot about it at the time, and one wonders if there may not have been notes for it as well as "heads". He must have had a clear idea about what he wanted to do, I think, while still in Salonika. The Bristol episodes in the Burghclere chapel would not require such feats of memory as the Salonika episodes.

In 1922, when he was staying with Henry Lamb at 10 Hill Street, Poole, he was drawing out these designs on the floor of an upstairs room as unhesitatingly as though he were writing a letter. It so happened that Louis and Mary Behrend called, and found him there at work on them. What followed is history. They were so impressed that they decided to do something about it. But what is not history is his reply when they made their first tentative proposal for the chapel: "Thank you very much, but it's not half good enough." I am indebted to Mary herself for this enlightening information. But would he have expressed such diffidence, one wonders, had he realised then that never was he going to have another such chance. Had it not been for the Behrends' persistence, there would not have been one. But he was lucky: between Henry, Mary and Louis, the miracle happened.

The architect of the chapel, Lionel Pearson, took the proportion of the building, arch spans and everything, from the little scale drawing Stan had done in Henry's room; and I expect that Pearson found, as I did when Stan used to lecture me about the exactitude necessary when measuring up from the scale drawings, that the scale was very precise. Stan would order canvases to 3/16ths of an inch sometimes.

My first introduction to the murals was at Hampstead, at the Vale of Health Hotel. Stan had finished the "Resurrection", and to fill in time while waiting for the chapel to be ready, he had painted the panel of the orderlies scrubbing. Compared with the "Resurrection", with its wealth of lovely colour and detail, this new painting did not, to my mind, look very good: it would have been hard to foresee, then, that it was the start of such a journey. From time to time I visited him at Burghclere, and saw many of the canvases for the arches and panels leaning against the wall. He was painting these on an easel, and having them placed in their positions as he finished them. He broke off occasionally to paint a landscape—"Cottages at Burghclere" (now in the Fitzwilliam), "Hilda and Unity with Dolls", and others.

I find it difficult to write about the murals, just as I once found it difficult when I was asked to say something about the Cookham Regatta picture. That was on an important occasion after he had returned to Fernley. The picture was partly unrolled and pinned up on the wall in our front bedroom. Outside the window, the fantails were still losing their foothold on the old roof of Oveys farmhouse. I felt uncomfortable and ill at ease, and out of the corner of my eye I could see that Stan, on a hard chair, was able to share what for him would have been a double discomfort. He was no great shakes at this sort of thing himself. Louis Behrend reminded me that if you wanted to hear him talking about his pictures, the time to do so was before and not after he had done them; then his excitement carried one into untold realms of visual experience, but after they had been painted, he was reduced to silence.

All the same, I wish I could explain these murals with the simple, almost childlike, spirit of my brother. Not that he ever attempted, when I was with him, to convey the secret of their spiritual quality. What was on the walls of the chapel can be regarded as a kind of screen by which artists both explain (get off their chests) and protect themselves. Here my brother is explaining what war felt like to him. Words, therefore, were few between us: all that was needed from him were winks, asides, smiles, gestures and pointings. He might, perhaps, have been pointing at the soldier cutting the other man out of a tangle of barbed wire: "You remember, Gil, those rolls of barbed wire we used to carry? —he was carrying one above his head when the strut broke and it all uncoiled and came pouring down on top of him." We were now looking at the "Resurrection of the Soldiers", and he would probably have denied any symbolism, however incidental, if it had been suggested. His whole concentration now would be centred on describing the incident and what a lovely thing it was to paint. He would put his finger across his mouth characteristically when drawing my attention to the lovely shape the turned back trouser-flaps of the man cutting the wire had made. Or I might have noticed the position of the man's hands inside the wire, to which he replied in an undertone: "Mysterious." He explained to me very carefully the flattened-out wagon on which the resurrected soldier lies prone, reading his name on his cross, while the driver nestles in sweet repose between the mules—as we had done as children between our parents in bed. The wagon had been hit by a shell, but instead of being blown to smithereens it had fallen apart intact. And it made the pattern he needed just there, leading on to the figure of Christ, receiving the crosses from the soldiers as simply as though they were handing in their kits at the end of the war. One feels that he dismantled that cart section by section in his mind.

The murals are not of war but of peace, and are imbued with the spirit of tranquillity which came with the Armistice. In them the war seems to have been pushed to one side by the realisation that Mill Lane was now only just round the corner.

It was a most rewarding experience just to look at this wall and let the ideas and patterns (and by patterns I mean the fringes of each section) gradually reveal themselves. If I were to try to tot them all up, I should still miss some. He himself would often take a canvas stretcher and frame one of these lesser incidents, to emphasise that within the larger whole each was there in its own right. It is worth doing this even with a reproduction of the wall, by cutting out little paper frames and isolating parts of the pattern: this helps to reveal how he worked, and at the same time gives an insight into the vividness of his mind. The part I particularly like isolating is the central incident of the mules, the collapsed cart, and the figure of Christ: I include the figure of Christ because the two mules are clearly intended to lead one on to Him. And so is the great soldier lying on his back on the top of the mass of crosses. Very soon one is aware of an avenue of incident leading inevitably to Christ. That is not only great designing, but is rational. My brother knew the difference between subtlety and obscurity.

It was Randolph Schwabe who once asked me if I thought he acted the incidents in his pictures. I had never felt this in the pre-war pictures; but when I recalled how he would explain some element of a picture with a gesture, I began to feel that he did physically as well as mentally work out his ideas. Take the "Ablutions" panel; all the figures are observed postures, the man having his chest painted with iodine, the orderly polishing the taps (who might well be him). And how admirably the back view of the man pulling his braces over his head has been timed to the purpose of the design. I often wonder whether this "Ablutions" panel was the one he was referring to when he said to a visitor: "Only Titian could have done that."

It is his power of statement that is so overwhelming, a power which, alas, often left him with too little time in which to convert it into paint. He told me on one occasion: "I put everything down." And on another: "I've got stacks of ideas"—almost complainingly.

And in the "Reveille" picture, in which we see soldiers rising from beneath their mosquito nets (a most effective pictorial idea) we are confronted with what one might almost regard as puritanical realism. He torments himself with a swarm of realistic flies in the top of the tent. Finding myself with something of the same situation in my painting on one of the walls at Holywell Manor, Oxford, in which I had introduced some rooks, I later got my "gun" and shot the lot. I don't think my brother would have been prepared to concede a single fly.

Here and there one comes on what might be the mood of an earlier period. Above the bivouacs in the "Firebelt" panel, in the midst of all the crowded activity, there is a little figure reminiscent of the figure above the wall in "Zacharias and Elizabeth". And when I consider the foreshortened figure of the man in the foreground, I wonder why he should have been so envious of what he called the "Story Boys" at Moor Hall, which had been taken over by a film company: "You know, ask them to draw a lion coming straight at you and they do it right away."

There is nothing in these murals to anticipate changes which were going to come later. He was still a naturalist as well as a realist, and once one has accustomed oneself to his habit of tilting his world up, as though he were climbing a kind of imaginative ladder to see what is going on behind, any feeling of disturbance disappears. Scarcely any of his compositions have skies; most of his designs are an enclosure. And in Cookham, too, our horizon was close, and our sky-line had the feeling to be found in so many of his pictures. The flat aspect to the south, he would say, was not cosy; and by "cosy" I think he meant "happy".

One is repeatedly caught up by the rich embellishment of his ideas, by his acute observation of people employed at their various tasks. He finds so many interesting shapes in these relationships. The human being is to some extent a controlled shape; attach him to his job and anything can happen. The man holding the unrolled puttee in the "Resurrection", or the isolated figure on the left in the "Camp at Kalinova"—one feels him everywhere in the miscellany of camp life behind the lines, re-living his own experiences among these busy troops—the jaunty little soldier stabbing at the rubbish with his bayonet, the soldier dragging his blanket behind him in "Kit Inspection", the dramatic figure of the camouflaged soldier in "Stand To". His people are never idling about; the man holding the tortoise, or the soldier resting between the mules, express repose.

These murals are so fresh, held together as they are not only by his acute powers of design and pattern—he would scoop an idea out of anything—but also by his continuing use of a very simple palette. Going round the walls of the chapel with him, it was abundantly clear that he loved painting them with every fibre in his body. The aftermath of all this, if one came on him unawares, was an impression of sadness—though not disappointment. But whatever may have been in my brother's mind when later he wrote: "I was, I feared, forsaking the vision and was filled with consternation," these murals are blameless. His routine was a seven day week. Most people found him approachable and lovable at this time. During the whole period he was working on them (1926–32), the door was never locked. Rodney Burn once found him perched high on the scaffolding reading Mark Twain. Sometimes the manner of his painting provoked adverse comments. He liked to imitate the voice of the General who expostulated: "To think of our dear boys." Whenever there was any hostility towards his pictures, he would grease down the ladder expertly and turn on the radiators. He told me that when people grumbled, he knew they were cold.

I think it was in 1929 that my brother Will returned from Switzerland on holiday, and Louis and Mary Behrend invited him to stay with them and to see the chapel. They had to go away and my brother stayed on alone. One day he invited Stan to breakfast. He informed the maid that his brother "will take coffee with me tomorrow". The maid, not understanding that in Switzerland "coffee" meant "breakfast", took it literally. Stan arrived, they sat down together, breakfast was brought in. For Will there was an egg, hot rolls, butter and marmalade—for Stan just coffee. Will thought it over and passed his rolls and marmalade to Stan. After further thought, he took the rolls and marmalade and passed the egg over. Now the situation was becoming intense. "No!" exclaimed Will, "*that* would be deception", and the egg made its journey back across the table, leaving Stan with his coffee. After this scene, typical of Will, Stan made his way to the kitchen to explain the mistake.

CHAPTER VIII

DROPPING DOWN OFF the causeway, I entered the village again on a lovely March morning in 1919. I felt like calling out this way and that, over walls and across gardens, to friends and relations as I went. Old Sammy Sandall wasn't there to return the call from his fireside; old age, not the war, had claimed him. But on the whole the village had not fared as badly as it might have done, and though I knew there had been losses, I was able to anticipate many happy reunions. Cookham would soon have back some of its pre-war character. I was happy.

The familiar voice of Annie Slack came from Shergold's shop as I passed. With her "Oh, it's Gil" and "How are you?" mingled with "Well, I never", and with a few more exchanges of this kind, I had made a promising beginning.

I was now nearly home. I had escaped so much, and my feelings as I turned the handle of the front door were of my good fortune to be back again.

I found Father at his usual place by the table, reading. Annie was upstairs with Mother, who was failing now, and stayed in bed for long periods; but her determined spirit brought her back into the life at Fernley at intervals, although she was never so active again as she had been before the war. When Father greeted me, he first asked "Which one are you?"; but after he had rubbed his eyes, he accepted my "Gil", as I bent over to give him his usual kiss on his forehead. As I did so he noticed a ribbon on my coat. I had to explain that it was the 1914–15 Star. After a few more generalities, Fernley returned to itself. There seemed little that one could talk about.

The first flush of excitement after the Armistice (which had found me guarding and losing Turkish prisoners in the

Sinai Desert) had now passed, and my feelings as I returned to the village were soon subject to some modification. That moment of *return*, which one had thought so much about when far away, had not quite come up to expectations. Except for an unlived-in feeling, however, everything at home appeared much as I had left it. Soon I might be hoping that Father would go out, so that I could strum the piano again.

But if there was something of an anti-climax here, it was quickly dispelled when, in answer to my enquiry, "Where's Stan?", Father replied, "He's up in Lambert's stables painting his war picture." And here I found him in one of the loose boxes. He greeted me with his usual, "Heh, well I'm blest." I seldom knew him to shake hands by way of greeting. The picture he was completing was "Travoys", and the canvas was too large for Fernley or for any of the other pre-war "studios". He was painting quite contentedly.

After a few exchanges, I left him, to take a walk round the village, and met one or two others who had already returned. One of them was Dilly Brooks, who had been under-gardener at "Tarry Stone House". Stan told me that in a spirit of enthusiasm he had asked him what his ambitions were now, to which Dilly had replied, "Tarry Stone 'ouse".

My brother told me, later, that when he returned, he had walked about the village in a positively cocky mood for a couple of days—a cockiness that arose from his happiness at being regarded as a man among men. He must have felt very pleased with himself, to have come through such testing experiences without place or favour.

The first rapture of his return was now over, and he had settled down again to complete "Swan Upping" and to paint his war picture. I know of no way other than his own simple method of direct painting that could have better bridged the gap of three years between starting and finishing "Swan Upping". It was a remarkable example of "invisible mending". Nor did the war appear to have disturbed his vision.

Financially I was the better off on our return. I had

received a gratuity of £16, entered in a Post Office Savings Book with a note from Lloyd George urging on me the necessity to save. But Stan had a commission from Muirhead Bone to paint his war picture. However, our greatest asset was still my father's continuing acceptance of our living at home on an unspecified financial arrangement.

We now began to notice various changes in the village. Coolings-off and re-alignments showed themselves. We looked out of our window early one morning, to see Parsons' cab drawn up outside Mr. Wooster's to take Emmie on the first stage of her journey to Australia and marriage—and we knew that our romantic walks down Mill Lane were over, an early casualty of the peace. Moreover, the old island feeling was going. Cookhamites were leaving as though it did not matter, and strangers were filling their places.

If the Fernley we had left had been "warlike" in its unpreparedness for war, the one we had returned to now seemed unsettlingly quiet, and so my brother and I bustled round to restore something of the old feeling. With Father reading by the lamp, and Stan back in the front bedroom reading and painting, I soon found myself again counting up my cards at cribbage and making the same mistakes about "his knob", if only for the sake of hearing my father's corrections again.

The village was filling up again as more and more of the men received their discharge. Annie Slack's shop was recovering its position as a social centre where one could spend whole evenings gossiping without having to spend any money.

We shed our khaki for civvy suits provided by a grateful Government, made to measure or near enough, and sent through the post in parcels ominously similar in appearance, as were the suits they contained. But there really was something rather charming about the Government's efforts to restore our individualities to us. We still looked very like one another but, in a gesture against uniformity, the suits came in three shades—navy blue, blue with a touch of purple, and purple with a touch of blue. Our overcoats we decided to sell for £1 apiece at Cookham Station; this was the regular price for this kind of garment in this kind of transaction.

With this final gesture it might have been thought that we had finished with the Army. But, just as a candle flickers up before dying out, so in a sense did we. Back on Cookham Moor we found ourselves confronted by a very excited and belligerent old gentleman with his arms full of armlets, who wanted to despatch us to vulnerable points on the railway. We did not know what was the matter. But when, later, we realised that we were now in the nature of shock troops sent to meet the first of the post-war crises, we decided not to parade any more. We were not a bit interested in strike-breaking.

That was the last occasion that Stan and I were concerned together in any form of public service.

Changing conditions, and the moods that were bringing them about, were making themselves felt in a number of ways now. That feeling of "neutrality" towards religion, about which my brother had complained, and which I always regarded as something to do with the Sabbath Day Act, with its many prohibitions against Sunday "indulgences", was becoming more widespread. These changes had been developing at home even before the war. When we had attended church or chapel, as the case might be, we then felt free for the rest of the day to carry on, indoors, very much as we did on any other day. And much the same sort of thing had, it seems, been going on under other roofs too. The Sabbath Day at Cookham must have been altering for longer than we had known, before the end of the war brought the change out into the open. But that is not to say that Cookham now acquired the characteristics of the Continental Sunday, which, from what we had heard as children, meant church in the morning and the fair on Cookham Moor afterwards. The village was still prepared to treat change as evolutionary rather than revolutionary. Until we left home, Sunday mornings continued to find Stan and me in our pew.

In the early summer of 1920, Henry Lamb wrote to Stan

from Stourpaine in Dorset, and we went down to stay at Durweston, a near-by village. Henry was staying with the Drapers at Havelins Farm, where he was painting his Manchester war picture, and we stayed at the Haskells and later the Winsors. We spent our time drawing heads and painting landscapes. These included "The Mill, Durweston", "The Harrow, Durweston", and a little landscape on wood, "Cornstooks", all by Stan and now belonging to Louis Behrend. My contribution included a little "Durweston Village" (Mrs. Harold Goring) and "Durweston Village" (Sir William Rothenstein). While at Durweston my brother must have been planning several of his most important compositions, which he was very soon to begin. His earlier method of completing each picture before making the drawing for the next was changing. But there was no Mill Lane at Durweston, and one has the feeling that it was a waiting period, which to some extent frustrated him.

He liked painting landscapes, but would become spiteful towards them if he felt that they were interfering with his other work, and would then roundly abuse what he sometimes called "these fiddling landscapes". "A good three-quarters" of his time, he declared in a letter to me, was "dictated by the buying public: landscape or portrait or still life". He complained then of "not understanding or liking this sort of work", of "being unable in any way to find *myself* in it". He vented this irritation on that innocent little picture of cornstooks in another letter to me, treating it as an example when explaining to me everything he hated most in painting this kind of thing; he conveyed the impression that when he set out to paint it, he did so with no other intention than to demonstrate this hatred. "I remember . . . deliberately choosing a nasty *unhomely* view," he wrote. "What could I not do if I had five clear years ahead of me in which to concentrate on what I wish to and feel I could do," he said in the same letter. He added, however, that there was more "hope and possibility" in earning a living this way than in teaching.

But his sense of humour was equal to most occasions. His

detachment was well demonstrated when "Hod Hill" was nearing completion. The picture had a lot of charlock in the foreground, painted by Stan with his usual love of detail. But when the farmer saw the picture, naturally enough he did not like the charlock. Next day when my brother arrived on the scene he found it had all been cut down. Stan enjoyed relating how the labourer who had done the job explained that the place looked better now. More surprising, Stan cut his down as well.

He would get very weary with the uncertain weather when landscape painting, and at moments of exasperation he would chase the clock round in an effort to catch one or other of its moods. Henry suggested to me one evening, when we noticed a light on Durweston Hill, that it might be "Cookham" finishing his picture.

In our painting at this time we relied very largely on sable brushes, and of this Henry rather disapproved. In answer to his criticism I made a little drawing of him dressed as a priest and holding aloft a couple of hogshair brushes, while Stan and I stood before him with sables pouring out of our bodies. It is called "Henry Casting Out Sables".

An example of my brother's courage arose while he was painting "Durweston Mill". Nearby, two of the "gentry" were shooting. We had grown to associate "gentry" with barbed wire, policemen, and charges of trespassing at Cookham, and at Durweston feudalism seemed even more powerful. Stan saw these sportsmen shoot a moorhen on the water, and this roused him. He introduced himself to them disarmingly enough with "That was a good shot", or something of the kind, and, before they could extricate themselves from this disguised pleasantry, he demanded to know why they had done it, and vigorously abused their manliness. His manner when annoyed could be quite fierce, and there were time when he was fortunate to get away with it. But he always did. Something shielded him: it may have been his size, or it might have been his bright red cheeks, or, as I think, it may have been due to a quality of "difference" that people sensed in him.

He seldom used strong language. Only once do I remember him doing so, and that was when he called me a "bloody dart thrower". That arose because he had seen me through the door of the Bell and Dragon Hotel having a glass of beer. By this time his antipathy towards "toffs" was intense, and as some of them were in the bar at the time, that was his way of expressing it. He was utterly unreasonable about such people, and quite incapable of viewing them dispassionately.

I spent many summers at Durweston with the Winsors, and occasionally Henry revisited the Drapers at Havelins Farm, from where he wrote to Stan, "Gil's down here putting in skies with one hand." Stan never returned. He had gone home to Cookham to start on some of his ideas.

When my brother began exhibiting, some of the critics spoke of "pre-Raphaelite influences". He himself was a little puzzled by such comments. Our historical sense regarding art was almost zero, and this was a period about which we knew nothing. There was the little reproduction of Rossetti's "Annunciation", certainly an impressive picture, hanging in our bedroom, and "in a way" Stan liked Fred Walker. And Will had visited "the Great Holman Hunt" in his studio. But there was no serious influence from the Brotherhood. How much my brother had read of them at the time I do not know. Very little, I imagine—but he read Ruskin, and so did Will. Rossetti came in through his poetry.

I have read something of their philosophy and general approach to their work recently, and find it very difficult to see much in common between them and my brother. He was anything but fanatical, and his ideas about God and his passionate feelings about love and joy never led him into didactic discussion—he discouraged it, sometimes with a jaunty little "Well, thank you very much for calling". But perhaps the influence of the Pre-Raphaelites was indirect. He saturated himself in the work of the Primitives which he found in the Gowans and Gray books. It was Masaccio's "St. Peter Healing The Cripple" that he first showed to me, and he had a Pisanello reproduction handy by his bed, to look at when he woke up.

His next important pictures after "Travoys" and "Swan Upping" were "Christ Carrying the Cross" and a strangely unCookhamish picture, the title of which I never knew, of figures on a stone bridge, which I could not identify, with a dog in the foreground. These were the last pictures he painted at Fernley until he returned there in 1959.

How oddly at variance with the mystical quality of his pictures his way of talking could be. He was very angry when he found that his title "Christ Carrying the Cross" had been changed to *His* cross. He repeatedly referred to what he called "the job", and to his religious pictures in this way as much as to the rest. He insisted that Christ was "just carrying the cross".

Many years later, when I was standing with him in our old pew at Cookham Church, looking at the "Crucifixion" hanging just above it, he remarked jocularly, "It's all right, Gil, you don't have to pray this time"—a reference to the fact that the last time we had been there together, so long ago, we did have to. Not irreverent, but characteristic. And in the midst of a talk which he gave later from the chancel steps at the Exhibition came the remark, "Our mother did all the washing, sheets and all", like a bolt from the blue. (Not accurate; Shackleton's Thistle Laundry did that.)

When he went on to talk about the "Crucifixion", most of his comments were about the men who had fixed the body on the cross. "The job" again; they "knew what they were doing", these men in the red brewers' hats, such as the man with the nails in his mouth who was hammering in a manner reminiscent of what we had seen when the horses were being shod. The event, the design, and the excitement of painting it, were all.

The break with Fernley was now nearer than either of us suspected. I was feeling that some kind of separate existence would be necessary for me if my strength was not to be sapped by the increasing excitements around me. But I did not know that my brother had any serious thought of leaving.

Certainly life at home was not getting any easier. And the war had hardened my mother to the fact of her sons' absence—with the exception of Will, we had all been in the Army.

Stan and I received an invitation from Harry and Margaret Slesser (Sir Henry and Lady Slesser) to spend a weekend at Cornerways. Soon after, Stan went to live with them, and I moved to Hampstead. Our introduction to the Slessers came through the Behrends, and their invitation to us was one after our own hearts. All we had to do was to stuff a suit of pyjamas into our pockets, walk along the tow-path to the Quarry Hotel, cross by the ferry, and pick our way among the many little islands of the Abbotsbrook Estate until we found the one on which Cornerways stood.

We all made short work of the usual formalities in getting to know one another; by the end of dinner they were all behind us. Quite early on we discovered that Harry could combine a deep regard for the mystics with a liking for Gilbert and Sullivan, and so could Stan.

After dinner we went out in the punt and drifted around innumerable islands which were linked together by little rustic bridges. In the cool summer nights this was a most enjoyable experience. Their homes concealed amidst shrubs and trees, friends and neighbours called across to one another from island to island.

Often there were long walks over the Chilterns and on to the Berkshire Downs, and arising out of these walks Harry created a walking fraternity, of which St. Ambularis was the patron saint. Besides Harry and Margaret, the members included Chesterton (non-ambulant), Deller (Sir Edwin Deller), A. L. Bacharach, Val Spalding, Roger Grant, Wilfred Evill, and Stan and me. Although it had its lighter side, its aims were friendship with an undertone of religion and philosophy in the beneficent conditions of fresh air, blue skies and wayside inns. Beer was the sacred beverage. There were fines for various offences, and the one which most strongly aroused the wrath of St. Ambularis was the drinking of cocoa. "Cocoa is a cad and coward, cocoa is a vulgar beast." Imagine, therefore, our amazement on learning that an empty cocoa tin had been found in Chesterton's rubbish bin.

He was duly charged with the crime. As many of us as could muster walked over to Beaconsfield for the trial, and were received must courteously by the accused before he took his place in the dock. Stan and I (the jury) thought it a pretty scurvy tiick of defending counsel (Evill) to attempt to put the blame on the servants. But before we could consider our verdict, Chesterton elected to withdraw his plea of not guilty and, to the consternation of the judge (Sir Henry Slesser), flung himself on the mercy of the court. All fines were paid in beer, and the fine in this case was a heavy one. The beer was served in the well of the court, after which we returned to Cornerways, singing as we walked of "the night we went to Birmingham by way of Beachy Head".

One member of the group was a Roman Catholic, another a High Anglican, and there were agnostics, atheists, and Stan and me. But the creed of St. Ambularis was never discussed. Stan's attitude and mine towards religion was now one of tolerance and respect for all creeds and complete independence from any denomination, but with that undertone of Christian ethics bred in us at home. Both Stan and I later visited the Third Church of Christ Scientist with the Carlines, but it had no appeal for us.

Shortly before leaving home, when on one of our long treks with Percy, as we were passing through Bisham we came on Eric Gill working on his crucifix in the village. He invited us into his rooms for a talk, and some little time afterwards he invited my brother to join him for a weekend at Ditchling. Gill was a very active Catholic, and I have no doubt that, in view of the nature of my brother's work at that time, he felt it could perhaps be canalised towards Catholicism. In this he was mistaken. Stan returned home in a state of angry resentment. Subsequently on two occasions I saw Gill at Northdean on business, and there were chance meetings too, but never was there the smallest enquiry after my brother. I wondered whether Gill had aroused my brother to a display of anger: as I have said, he could be a good deal rougher than one might expect.

Having come through the war unscathed, Stan now bought himself a motor-car. Soon he was driving to London and getting into great difficulty in finding his way out of Piccadilly Circus once he had found his way into it. He did not keep the car for long, for two reasons. He had taken into his employment a rather large Swiss lady, whom he used to refer to as "Miss Swiss Alps". She quickly acquainted herself with the mechanics of motoring, and thereafter my brother found that the car was frequently unavailable when he wanted it. There was some bitterness in this. His other reason for getting rid of it was on account of a collision with a lorry in Marlow Road, Maidenhead. He described the scene with his customary attention to detail. His car finished up half way through the fence surrounding Kidwells Park. When the rest of the party had scrambled out it was realised that Mrs. Carline was still inside, seemingly in extremis. Some of the crowd got her out, and she revived sufficiently to meet with strong protests a policeman's intention to send for an ambulance. She was a Christian Scientist, and wanted someone to ring up Lady Astor for a Christian Science healer. In the face of this, the policeman stated that he didn't want to interfere with anybody's religious scruples. Finally, the car was jacked up, and my brother returned to his seat at the wheel, and was ignominiously dragged back to Cookham on the back wheels.

Before leaving Cornerways he painted "The Last Supper", which for a time formed the altar piece in Harry Slesser's private chapel in the boat house. While painting it, he had a very odd experience. He had been looking round in the malt houses for a setting for the picture. They had long since been closed, but were now in course of reconstruction. The workmen invited him to look under one of the floors, and there he saw, picked out by a shaft of light from a ventilator, an almost life-sized skeleton cut out of cardboard. The men were puzzled.

One possible explanation occurs to me. As children we

had been frightened by the report of the periodical appearance of what was known as "Waller's ghost". The manager of the malt houses, Mr. Waller, employed as maltster a morbid fellow and, judging by some of his nicknames, a sinister character as well. Mr. Waller had a glass eye, and whenever he met the Spencer family out walking, he performed a little turn of greeting us with "Morning, morning—morning, morning all". He lived with his family in a long rambling house which lay almost hidden behind a cedar tree. Twice a widower, he had married for the third time. Later, the family's peace began to be disturbed by noises on the upper floor of the house—noises that sounded like someone walking about overhead and opening and shutting drawers. One of the daughters was terrified to see what she believed to be her own mother in front of a mirror combing her hair; as the apparition turned to look at her, she fled. The report that "Waller's ghost" was about continued to disturb the village for some years. It was finally "laid" after some boys, playing in the ditches down Odney, had come upon the body of the eccentric maltster lying in about ten feet of water. A complete outfit of women's clothes, and even a wig, were then found in his cottage adjoining Mr. Waller's. Presumably it was he whom the daughter saw and mistook for her mother. The cardboard skeleton under the floorboards may have been another example of his macabre fancy. Stan and I both thought it was, but he carried its secret with him into the pool at Odney.

CHAPTER IX

I HAD NOW MOVED to Hampstead. With Henry Lamb at the Vale of Health Hotel and the Carlines at 47 Downshire Hill, there was no recurrence of homesickness. The Carlines lived in one of two semi-detached houses which held one another up at the corner of Keats Grove. It had a balcony that looked and was very dangerous to stand on. Soon after I began visiting there, a lion's head made of iron fell from the high guttering along the roof, smashing into the terrace at the back of the house, but not injuring anybody. The family interestedly gathered round, turned it this way and that, with an occasional glance up at the roof, and then carried it off to the stables to take its place with a veritable museum of oddments.

The time had not yet arrived when the spacious basement kitchen came into use: meals were still taken in the dining-room. The house was full of furniture of character and interest: however many rooms there had been at the Shrubbery, No. 47 would have absorbed the contents of twice the number. Mrs. Carline would have seen to that. There was scarcely an inch of wall that was not taken up by a picture, all of them by "Da" except for a drawing of a swan made by Dick at an early age, and a lovely Lely and a huge Ghirlandaio. Da was not an Academician—though it is true that he got his second version of "Autumn" into the Royal Academy after having found out what was wrong with the first. His life, his kindliness and his politeness covered the walls. His family grew up on his canvases; one could look back to the time when the beauty of Mrs. Carline was scarcely out of its teens. All their holidays—and the Carlines were inveterate travellers—were there, brought right up to date when Stan and I went with them to Seaford and later Stan went with them to Bosnia.

When the Carlines were on the move, and they generally were about June, their lives were very different. Luxury hotels on the tourist routes were not for them. Strange, dusky photographs revealed them looking thoroughly natural in what appeared to be elongated stables in Andorra, an advance upon earlier holidays in Swiss chalets. When they went to Bosnia, Mrs. Carline, who had a genius for assimilation, was quickly off the mark with her shopping bag in the town. It was here that one Kusmitch introduced himself to them. He had a simple story to tell of lovers separated by lack of funds. At once it was decided to pay his travelling expenses, and amidst many salutations he departed. When he returned, his only comment in answer to their enquiries was: "I did thrash her."

On summer evenings we had our meals on the terrace in the garden, which had a strong Continental feeling about it. Mrs. Carline's gardening was again of a highly individual kind. She sowed seeds as though she were feeding the birds. She strewed the garden with Corots, and even an occasional Cezanne would emerge. We would move about among them playing a particularly unorthodox form of croquet.

Hilda, with her auburn hair—she bore some resemblance to Whistler's Symphony in White—was a sight to stir anyone who was romantically inclined. She was no ordinary girl: she always seemed to be thinking very hard about something, though this did not inhibit her enchanting sense of humour and fun. She was perhaps a little remote, but when she talked she was always interesting. Her comment about Stan was true of her too: "When Stanley says something, somehow it isn't the same as when anyone else says it."

Croquet would often continue until well after dark, aided by candles placed at the hoops. Afterwards we all retired to the drawing-room upstairs, once more to dwell among the pictures and to drink tea, eat dripping cakes, and argue until well after midnight. The talk might be about Sydney's or

Dick's latest finds at the Cumberland market—little Easter Island effigies, Ming horses, Chinese dishes, bits of valuable Gobelin tapestry which only needed sending to the wash, and a dragon worked in very fine gold wire on a red cloth, which Dick spent many hours repairing. But whatever the subject, the discussion was always enlivened by humorous banter and touches of cynicism.

Their studio was at 14-A, opposite an old chapel, and here the family divided themselves into departments. Hilda occupied the long passage, and here she painted a Slade picture and many others which proved her to be an artist in her own right; but owing to the location of her "studio" she was known as the "passage artist".

Here was a family which, like us, was professional. It was all painting with them, except that Hilda had played the harp. We know this because of one of Da's paintings of her: and the harp filled a corner of the drawing-room, with half its strings gone. Amidst all the "whirlings around", as Mrs. Carline called everything, she too, after Da's death, found energy enough to turn to painting, and of all the group—Sydney, Dick, Hilda, Gertler, Henry Lamb, John Nash, James Woods, Richard Hartley, John Duguid and a host of others, including Stan and myself, she was the only one to achieve a one-man show in Paris.

When Mrs. Carline had her show in Paris it was sheer glamour, but for us the exhibiting of pictures had to be something more than that if we were going to survive. By now (1920) we were both members of the New English Art Club and were showing there. It had a fine record. A photograph of the selection jury at their work reveals a trestle table set up in some kind of shed: only three of the members are seated, and no more chairs seem to be available. At one end of the table a workman is displaying a picture, while at the other end sits Mr. Winter, the Secretary, whose terms of service were, I suspect, for the duration of the exhibition only. What has puzzled me about this photograph is that, in a setting of such simplicity, a top hat rests on the table. Who could it have belonged to?

Certainly not to Augustus John, standing just behind it and wearing a sweater and a wide-awake hat. McColl stands nearby and behind him Steer. Rothenstein is sitting on a corner of the table and among the rest are Brown, Orpen, MacEvoy, Russell, Lees, and, overlooking them all, Tonks. Could that hat have belonged to Sickert?

At the Post-Impressionist Exhibition in 1912, my brother had exhibited "John Donne Arriving in Heaven" and two drawings. But it was the NEAC that introduced him now to the public.

Art in those days was a very exclusive profession. To a considerable extent, artists lived by occasional purchases, made by a handful of interested friends rather than clients. Artists helped one another as well. There is a letter from my Father to Henry Lamb expressing his deep gratitude for what he was doing for us. And to Henry's name could be added those of Muirhead Bone, Francis Dodd, Gwen Darwin and John Dodgson. Neville Lewis commissioned me to paint his wife's portrait. But the real test was yet to come, and with my brother's first showing of his pictures he established a position from which there was no recession.

Nevertheless, in so exclusive a circle a young artist had got to find other outlets. Tonks' idea that an artist should show only at one gallery—in this case the NEAC—was too restricted to pay the bread-book the whole year round, and we set out to woo the other dealers.

Wooing dealers in those days was a ticklish undertaking. They took risks—not big risks, but risks all the same. They paid out monthly cheques, though not large ones. Mine was £12 a month. Agreements were signed in which one surrendered the whole of one's output to them to sell at 25 per cent.

It worked very well and enabled young artists, remembering their "pledge" to Tonks, to go on as though they had not broken it. Art criticism in those days was directed to the pictures and to nothing else. The dealer's own judgment was also involved as a guarantee. There was a trilogy of responsibility: it was not left to the artist alone to establish his integrity.

My brother continued for a while at Cornerways and stood in no need of these props, and I continued at Denning Road. I visited Henry often in his studio while his Lytton Strachey portrait was leaning against the wall.

One night he played the whole of the Diabelli Variations to us. He also treated me to a season ticket for all the Beethoven quartets (played by the London String Quartet). Towards the end, when I was getting into deep water, he nudged me and whispered, "It's all right, Gil, there are only four more to go." He was very impressed with the playing of Warwick Evans.

After a visit to the South of France, I went down to Cornerways to show Stan what I had done. He was still working on "The Last Supper". He stayed on there for some little time and then, in response to an invitation from Muirhead Bone, he went to stay near Petersfield, to give painting lessons to young Stephen Bone and to paint his picture of "The Unveiling of the Cookham War Memorial". He was troubled by the un-Cookhamish feeling of the top left-hand corner of this picture, the first major work he had attempted away from home. (Cornerways had been a "home from home". Both "Christ Carrying the Cross" and "The Last Supper" were impregnated with his strong feeling for *place*.)

Earlier, when Bone had visited us at Cookham with Henry Rushbury and Francis Dodd, and found us in our usual mood of complete confidence in one another, he had expressed some misgivings about "these young Spencers". And now we were leading a very vagrant kind of existence among our friends. Studios did not play a very important part in our development. Bedrooms, attics, barns, sheds and stables, these had been our workrooms from the beginning, and anything bordering on a real studio would have felt all wrong. I believe we would have preferred to paint bad pictures in a nice cosy sunny room to good ones in a north light.

When I think of my brother's output, his painting paraphernalia was extraordinarily slight. He had no stocks of paints, no drawers full of materials, no drawing benches with high chairs and electric lamps. Mostly he contented himself with a corner of a table, or squatted on the floor. And there always was the element of slipping-up-to-Mr.-Bockham's-to-get-another-brush about him.

Be that as it may, before he left the Bones there had been an occasion when Lady Bone had felt constrained to urge humility upon him. "Be a little more humble, Stanley", she had said, but he was not disposed to accept the admonishment "in all humility". And so there was an interlude which he spent at No. 1 The Square, Petersfield, while he made his plans to go and live with Henry Lamb at Poole, where the events I have already described took place.

In his acceptance of hospitality he was almost arrogant at times, as though he knew he was conferring as well as receiving. I think everyone would have conceded this, and in Henry he could not have found a more understanding host. He knew Stan thoroughly, and when he once referred to him as "desperate" he was very near the truth. There was no repose in Stan. On one occasion when Pansy (Lady Pansy Lamb) telephoned to Henry and could scarcely hear what he was saying, Henry explained to her that the noise in the background was only "Cookham" threatening to smash up the piano.

But one had no need to take these outbursts too seriously. What was often more interesting about them was their cause. There was, for instance, the argument about sailing weather. Henry had bought a small sailing boat, which the old salts around the harbour had described as a coffin, claiming that the centre board was so heavy that if the boat capsized it foundered. As a family we were notorious at sensing danger. My brother was courageous but if he thought something was foolhardy it riled him. Outside the dining-room window was a cypress tree which Stan had learned to regard as a wind-gauge, contending that its slightest movement meant that it would be very rough in Poole harbour. When one afternoon Henry expressed his intention of going sailing after tea, Stan pointed to the cypress: "There you are, Henry. Did you see that? There, it nearly blew over!" To have tried to pacify him by suggesting that he need not go would only have increased his annoyance: that was not the point at all. We were cursed with an over-awareness of danger and his aim was to convert Henry to a like state of mind. If he failed, it meant capitulation, which was the case this time. We all went sailing.

After my return from France, on an introduction from Stan I went to Caversham to live with a Slade friend of his, the artist T. S. Nash, and his wife. I was there for about eighteen months, and from there, with Stan and T. S. Nash looking over the pictures, I organised my first one-man show at Goupil. It certainly was not vanity that made me take this course: but I was having to fight my own battles now.

Later, at the invitation of Lady Ottoline Morrell, I went to live at Garsington. All the other painters, poets and writers who visited the manor called her "Ottoline", but we never did. Our sense of station was strong in us. That grown-up way of Christian-naming and "old manning" we could never manage, and there are letters in existence from both of us to Henry, asking if he really wished us to stop calling him "Mr. Lamb". Stan would occasionally stay at the Manor, take a look at what I was up to, and note that I was being very happy, lodging at Blenham Cottages and dividing my time between the Oxford life, the Manor, and my other close friends, Capt. Woodruffe and family.

It was shortly before I left Caversham that Mother died in May 1922. The chairs in the drawing-room were now all occupied with wreaths. Will came over from Thün, and he and Father, in their black frock coats and carrying their hats, examined the cards and exchanged memories of friends and relations.

She is buried in Cookham Cemetery.

In a letter to my sister Florence, Will writes of her: "I like, too, to think of Mother in earlier days—the beautiful first half of my life when I was living at home . . . I like to remember that once when I was playing Schumann's Papillons Opus 2 in the dining-room at Fernley and had just reached the fourth number, Mother came in from the kitchen and almost danced to it. My best memories of Mother are all at Cookham."

To us, of course, this picture of her belonged to a period we were too young to know. But if she no longer danced, the spirit had remained.

Once she had vied with Father in the writing of poetry: when our old cat "Stray" died, she expressed her feelings in a compact little poem which she sent to my brother in Cologne, and in his acknowledgement he wrote that it was "almost telegraphic". In the family efforts at oratorio, she could fill in gaps by switching from one part to another, sometimes making a gallant attempt at the bass.

Her Wesleyanism brought with it some taboos, but she knew something of birth control and imparted this knowledge on one occasion. She was conscious of "station" in life, and occasionally we were made aware of this. She had presence, and a dignity which came naturally to her on every occasion. Her interests were all in her family, and she never allowed the severe discomforts of a long illness to come between her and us.

Stan's next move was to become the tenant of Henry's studio at the Vale of Health Hotel. There is extant a rather confused letter from Stan in which he accounted to Henry for a disbursement he had made to the redoubtable Mrs. Gray, the landlady. Incidentally, I had been with Henry when he bought 10 Hill Street, Poole. The writing of the cheque (a four figure one) had been a big moment for him: he had remarked: "With all my wordly goods I thee endow," and I would not be surprised if this were not true. Every penny he owned he earned, and yet there never was a more ruthlessly independent painter. He was very selective when portrait painting. It was not the faces that primarily interested him, and in conversation one discovered that he had all sorts of odd reasons for agreeing to paint his subjects.

He could be very helpful to other painters with his comments—that is, if they could stand up to an honest opinion —and had a subtle way of egging one on at the same time.

With Stan things were different: you were either in heaven or in hell. It was a comfort that he usually reserved his powder for big game. Henry told me he had said of one of Henry's pictures that it had not got a centre, and added ruefully, "Of course, he was quite right". And there was the time when he said that one of my pictures ("Strayed Sheep") was a hullabaloo about nothing. His criticisms were seldom analytical: they were enthusiastically for or against.

He was not long in residence at the Vale of Health before he had one of those odd experiences that continually seemed to befall him. Arriving home to find the door locked, he rang the bell, as any sane citizen would. When the door opened he found himself confronted by a furiously angry landlord—the formidable Fred Gray, whom he had not seen before—holding a revolver in his hand. He gave Stan a tremendous dressing down before allowing him to pass up the endless carpetless stairs to bed. Stan cried, he told me. Next morning he sought the sympathy of Mrs. Gray, who explained that Fred had a lot to cope with, what with one thing and another, and that there was always a lot of money on the premises on Saturday nights. Reassured, Stan returned to his studio to start "The Resurrection".

In this work we have the last of the pictures in which Cookham played so important a part, and was so at one with his vision. Up till now it was not possible to separate the vision and the setting. His later pictures showed a lessening of this fusion.

Cookham churchyard had been for us, as children, I would not say a playground, but a place which it was a pleasure to be in. The significance of the graves naturally had no meaning for us then. I do not mean that we played hide and seek there, but we peered happily between heavy railings round the vaults of the grandees, and down a dark chasm where one vault had crumbled away. There was plenty of variety in the tombstones. Our father shared our pleasure and could often be found there reading or resting on sunny evenings, and telling passers-by how he "loved warmth".

It was a special treat for us to be taken by him down to the old stunted elm just inside the kissing gate at twilight to hear the owls "snoring". One evening he tapped the tree with his stick to "rouse" them, which he did to such effect that he shook one of the little owls off its perch and it fell to the ground. We felt it might have come from another world, this fluffy ball of the palest of yellows with its staring eyes; and the owl may have believed it was the resurrection morning. But death did not haunt our thoughts at all at this place.

As a family we were attracted to churchyards in general. On our long walks we always visited the churches and looked round the yards. Many was the time that we doted on the alabasters in Bisham Church. On one tombstone in Cookham churchyard there was an account of the fate of a local carrier which ran something like this:

> "Scarce does the sun each morning rise and set its evening ray,
> Without some human sacrifice, some tragic scene, display,
> Well could he drive the courser fleet which oft he drove before,
> When turning round a narrow lane he fell to rise no more."

The tombstone inscriptions were always a source of interest to our elders, and to us too as we grew older.

But one thing we abhorred was cemeteries. Cookham churchyard, Bisham churchyard, Hurley churchyard, Bray churchyard—but Maidenhead cemetery, never. Had we been told that it was heaven itself, nothing would have got us through those gates.

For me the churchyard is the keystone of the "Resurrection". Father used to assert that Milton preferred the Devil because it gave him greater scope in which to develop his arguments. But my brother here, except for one reference to the damned, which is a reminder of James Woods' "Resurrection of the Good and the Bad" (1913), prefers to depict all the figures rising from their graves in a state of blissful anticipation of taking their places on the *Marguerite*, moored in Bell Rope meadow to embark them for heaven. They have, one feels, avoided the Last Judgment : it is a picture of the innocent.

He never was much occupied with the wickedness in the world. Not that he was not aware of it; in experience he was wordly. But in his pictures he could pass it by. All signposts pointed the same way for him, to bliss and joy. Suffering he experienced too as time advanced, but had he painted a "Last Judgment" for Llandaff Cathedral (he was asked to do so, and paid a visit to the cathedral with Epstein, whose "Christ in Glory" had also been commissioned), the late "Crucifixion" would have been the pattern of it with its terrifying ignorance of—rather than indifference to—brutality.

A crowding of ideas was largely responsible for the lack of finish in his later work. He must at times have been almost startled by the intruding demands of new ideas, which even in the small hours would often get him out of the camp bed in which he slept towards the end of his life at Cliveden View (with all his drawings around him, pinned on the walls, or spread on the floor).

The many versions of the "Baptism of Christ" might have seemed to have expended its possibilities, but his own version offered another answer. He placed Christ up to his neck in water in one of the holes in Odney Pool, with his arms lying on the bank, just as we sometimes did when trying to pull ourselves out. St. John the Baptist he placed not beside him but standing on the bank above him. There was nothing pedantic about this: it is all practical, and thoroughly worked out.

Returning to "The Resurrection at Cookham", on my visits to him at the Vale of Health there was the same attitude in him as I have already described in writing of the Burghclere Chapel.

I think he enjoyed the sound of praise but I don't think he was much affected by its content; he was so concentrated on his own ideas. I don't believe he ever altered anything as the result of criticism. He was tenacious to the point of appearing to be obstinate.

The most I ever heard from him in self-deprecation was "I pinched that". When he did say that, I think he enjoyed doing so. He said it in a tone of bravado. When talking to me about one of the figures in "Christ Preaching at Cookham Regatta" he said, "I pinched that from your 'Miller' ". He had praised that picture of mine, and what he said was a concession he liked to make to other artists from time to time. "I went to the National Gallery to see how to paint the fur collar," he told me when we were looking at the portrait of Jack Martineau in his robes as Chairman of the Brewers' Company. His wife told me that Stan had looked at Tintoretto and said that he thought that *his* fur was just as good.

He worked on an odd intuitive principle. Theoretically it was: As A is related to B and B is related to C, C will be related to A. When arriving at Z, all will tie in successfully. It was the purest act of faith—which must play a part in all mural painting, particularly when the work goes round corners and at times is behind you. I never noticed him working from any colour scheme and, as he developed, he tended more and more to paint the colours he saw.

"The Resurrection in Cookham" is a huge easel picture. It was while he was painting it that he married Hilda Carline at Wangford in 1925. Later I was invited to join them there. We stayed in a cowman's cottage and painted out of doors. Stan painted "Trees and Chicken Coop, Wangford", Hilda painted a long landscape, and I painted "The Windmill, Wangford".

In the evenings we would sit around, Stan as usual at a corner of the table either reading or looking at reproductions. Occasionally something of an inquest was held on the pictures. When this happened, Hilda took the lead. I was content to praise, and Stan sometimes declared that all an artist wanted was praise. But Hilda knew the pitfalls of this sort of attitude and would brace herself by directing her attention to my picture while Stan continued reading. For a time with her head on one side she would remain silent. Then the overwhelming comment might come, "Somehow it isn't you".

A letter came from Lucy Silcox, headmistress of St. Felix School, asking Stan to paint her portrait. From time to time he would aim at involving me in his commissions, and when this happened there was nothing I could do about it. This time it was arranged that he, Hilda and I should work together.

We all trooped in together. There was nothing of the professional portrait painter about us. We were shown into a large room which was very dark because Miss Silcox had all the windows curtained so that the gay and inquisitive young ladies of St. Felix would not know what was happening. But of course they knew, and Marjory Lily, the art mistress, who had done much spade work to persuade Lucy to have the portrait done, told us so.

The light did not improve, and the painting went on for rather a long time. But I was thinking how well my brother was getting on when to our surprise, and Lucy's consternation, he took his canvas from the easel, placed it on the floor, and with a piece of rag proceeded to scrub—it was not a professional scrapedown—almost everything off the canvas.

Lucy's reactions were sharp, and we went no further with the portrait. But there was a happy sequel later when she bought "St. Francis".

Shortly after Stan and Hilda had returned to Hampstead, Shirin was born at the Vale of Health Hotel.

In 1927 he held his first one-man show at the Goupil Gallery and, with "The Resurrection" taking up the whole of one wall, it was an outstanding event. The excitement of it all affected him in a very touching way. I am sure he was alive to his status, but it produced no change in his demeanour, he seemed to wander about amidst it all as though he were the medium and not the creator.

But he liked describing the dismantling of "The Resurrection", its being lowered by a rope down the outside of the Vale of Health Hotel, the busy workmen, the scaffolding and the hoist, and the "Keep her clear, George" and "Hold it! Hold it!" from the men in the street below.

With some of the money he made from this exhibition he brought a Bechstein piano. He subsequently described to me a visit from a piano tuner. He looked "very grand", Stan said, indicating that he wore something akin to a frock coat. After he had completed the tuning he advised my brother that the keys were a little stiff in the upper and lower registers. Stan explained to him that his playing was almost entirely restricted to the middle register. There was a pause. Then the tuner said: "In that case, Mr. Spencer, you had better just flick it with a duster every morning."

His playing was certainly restricted to a very few pieces, but what he did play, with his limited technique, he played impressively. He learnt a Beethoven sonata with Muriel Harter which enabled him greatly to improve his technique as well. His prestos now left the realms of his andantes. When he played, he always looked down, and the precision with which he went to his positions on the keyboard was noticeable.

As a family we were brought up to abhor wrong notes. The home edict was that if you could not play the right notes at the right tempo, then for God's sake play them adagio until you could. On one occasion we were playing at a friend's house. Our hostess, a bustling sort of woman, took over the keyboard, and at molto presto proceeded to smear it all over with wrong notes. As she was a peeress, Stan and I just looked at one another. We were experts at the language of the eyes.

My father died in January 1928 in his 82nd year. He had lived to see my brother established at the top of the tree, but he was too old by then to have exploited this as he would have liked.

For some years he had retired behind his books by the lamp, and seemed to have made his peace. He was a Victorian, and a Victorian father into the bargain. By present-day standards that would have been regarded as a difficult father, but by our standards it only meant that he could be critical. He never believed in repressive methods, but he certainly went all out for victories by quotation and argument. Although we did not come much into his life until he was in his early sixties, he never allowed "little discrepancies" in the matter of age to intervene in these mêlées. He had his taboos. He hated idling, in himself and in others. Intrigues and the pettinesses of life were no part of him. I think Stan inherited his hard-chair reading from him. He had a strong sense of humour: he was the butt of all our family jokes, and accepted them in very good part and with a chuckle.

He certainly was very much the father of Stanley in his powers of concentration. His habit of quoting, his explanations of the Bible to us, his delight in imparting his knowledge, and his many odd Victorianisms, built him into an exciting father for anyone with a developing mind.

He had faults, which those with longer memories did not forget. There was his seeming lack of active concern when called upon to face financial difficulties. But he was not too proud then to attempt his own characteristic means of solving such problems. His successes in finding patrons was remarkable: he received only one rebuff, as far as I know—that was when he wrote to the Duke of Westminster inviting him to open up his London house, out of season, so that Will might give his recitals there. When he wrote to the Queen about Horace's conjuring, he afterwards proudly displayed Lord Stamfordham's reply: either he really believed that his letter had reached the Queen or, if he did not, he meant others to.

He spent much of his old age sitting just outside his front gate, from which he occasionally took a walk round the village. Then he would sometimes stop to look into a perambulator and say, "Bless their little hearts". His compassion for babies remained with him all his life.

There were stories he greatly liked to tell. One of them was of an occasion when, at a funeral, the horses drawing the hearse bolted. And this story was quite closely re-enacted at his own funeral, when one of the cabs, turning a corner in a narrow lane, was in collision with a motor-car. That the accident was not worse was due more to the skill of the driver of the horse than of the car. As it happened, there was a serious influenza epidemic at the time, which prevented all save my brother Percy and myself from attending the funeral, and thus we had a cab to spare, and it was into this cab, which received the brunt of the crash, that Percy and I had put the undertakers.

In giving this account of Father's funeral I hope I shall not be accused of levity. I am sure that had it happened to anyone else, he would have been irresistibly tempted to tell the story himself.

The next important event in my life certainly had its comic side. When, shortly after Father's death, I told Mrs. Carline that I was going down to Bagley Wood near Sunningwell, she asked me to get some black enamel and to repaint the lettering on the family tombstone in the churchyard there. I was going down to draw a portrait of J. G. Bradshaw for his daughter Ursula. The tombstone was a large one, and Ursula helped me, and a great amount of lettering needed attention. By the time we had completed this task and I had completed the drawing, Ursula and I had decided to marry.

When her father asked her whether I could support her, she confidently replied "No!" Later, when we were sitting in the Fava Restaurant discussing ways and means of making ends meet, Ernest Rhys, who was sitting at a nearby table reading *The Ancient Mariner* and overheard our conversation, came over and gave us the book as a wedding present, inscribing it "You will if you will it", and dating it—December 27, 1930, three days before our marriage.

I had met Ursula some years before at the Ruskin School at Oxford, where she was not only my pupil but Stan's as well. And as this was the only school at which Stan ever submitted to a routine appointment, some account of it would not be out of place.

Some years before 1930, Sidney Carline had succeeded the ageing MacDonald as the Ruskin master of drawing at Oxford. But life classes were not permitted then in the Ashmolean. Sidney Carline arranged to take over a local school run by Albert Rutherston and Vera Poole, and under his direction the Ruskin School took on a new life. The fig leaf was on the way out, though not without a fight. The staff was enlarged and now included Vera Poole, John Nash, Richard Carline, Stan and myself. It was a jolly school but it was not long before Sidney began shortening the distance between the present and the future. A divided school was inconvenient; it was far better that it should all be under one roof. His methods were subtle. He would drop hints and take soundings at Oxford tea parties. These subtleties soon reached the ears of Dr. Farnell, the Vice-chancellor, and the battle was joined. For some time we worked in the atmosphere of a frontier outpost. By skilful arrangement, nudes could be draped at the shortest notice. In the end Carline gained the day, the Cornmarket School was closed, and the fig leaf was banished from the Ashmolean.

For the teachers, money was left in a drawer—and was spent jollificating with the pupils. But it was a serious school, and quite a number of efficiently trained students came out of it who are still painting and drawing. Its policy was based on the Slade and its spirit of dedication. Teaching in those days was a happy experience. We were believed, our little demonstration drawings were kept. It almost amounted to hero worship and we lapped it up. We were treated with great kindness. There were invitations to Austin and Vera Poole's, to the Cartwrights at Sutton Courtney, to Hilda Harrison's at Boars Hill, and to Wick Hall, the mysterious home near Radley of the Dockar-Drysdales. Through his daughters, Helen and Betty, we visited Canon Cook at Christ Church, and he read Barnes' poetry to us.

And finally, business was good. The indefatigable Nellie Price, secretary of the Arts Club, organised shows for us. And when my turn came round, I opened a letter one morning that seemed to have been jotted down on a piece of paper torn out of a milk book. At a first reading, I thought it said that Sir Michael Sadler would buy my whole show, but closer scrutiny revealed that he wanted only eight!

After my marriage, when Ursula and I set up home in a flat at the home of A. H. Fox Strangways, I saw less of my brother. We wrote only when something happened which was "family" in feeling; the letters I have of his are lively in their descriptions of such happenings.

His next move, to Lindworth at Cookham, took place around 1932, shortly after which he entered a nursing home at Reading for a serious operation. My wife and I went down to Reading to see him, and on our way we slipped into Whiteleys to buy him a dressing-gown. Knowing his little ways about such things, we did not spend an inordinate amount of time considering pattern and colour. But he would take a momentary pride in a new suit.

We found him in characteristic mood, a mixture of petulance, humour, and complete divorcement from his physical situation. He described to us with considerable attention and interest an instrument that he had drawn, from the directions of Mr. Joyce, the surgeon, that was to be used in the operation. Clearly he was fascinated by it. His petulance arose as the result of a visit by some "high up". The visitor wielded power and that was enough. This Stan hated. He might have wielded power himself, but never did so. Complete freedom for the individual was his creed, and any restrictions on it he found intolerable. Many years ago a Frenchman wrote to us, "The Spencers are good Liberals and they were taught by their sister Annie."

I don't think he ever wore the dressing-gown, but later, I am convinced, he lent it to St. Francis. I liked "St. Francis" very much. I recognised in it a difference from the rapture of innocence in the earlier pictures. But such innocence could not survive close and ever closer communion with humanity. What perhaps is surprising is that in the change he retained his vision, and could still regard the life around him with such vivid and unimpaired imagination.

With his deepening experience he became more concerned with the psychological aspects of design, and "St. Francis" is an early example of his more deeply personal, if perhaps less comfortable, mode of expression. Distortion for a purpose is a fundamental canon in art, and in this picture, so much more expressive of this strange mystic than the "soft answers" so many painters have given, my brother never lost sight of the spirit of St. Francis.

But the rejection of the picture by the jury of the Royal Academy brought about a psychological change of a quite different order. He became a publicist as well as a painter. Circumstances forced this on him, and he responded with enthusiasm and affability, punctuated at times with disconcerting candour. And now the public was discovering, as we had known for so long, that as well as being a painter he was a personality.

I have seen one or two pictures by him which need not be available for general circulation for the present—though not on account of obscenity. But these are not the works that brought about the censure of Sir Alfred Munnings. But I happen also to have seen two of the drawings that did. They are delightful little drawings, and when he showed them to me at Cliveden View he described how they came into being. He had visited a privy down a cottage garden, and on opening the door he found not one but three seats of varying heights (these family privvies were more common than we knew). So what he did in the drawings was to put all three into occupation simultaneously. There they were, father, mother and little child, looking rather like three up-turned cabbages on a bench, most beautifully drawn and making a lovely pattern.

After he had settled at Lindworth, and I had gone to Oxford to paint the legend of Balliol, my wife and I made periodical visits to Cookham. Once, when I wrote to tell him that I would be coming for a night, he said in his reply: "I told Mrs. Barnes (his old servant) you would be coming on Wednesday and Thursday. There was no need for me to tell her to prepare the room for you. Her activities in connection with it almost began at once. I could hardly get her to take my breakfast things away first."

In the evening we sat together (Hilda was away). The room was strewn with his drawings, canvases and books. A corner of the table was cleared for a simple meal, with the fried bread which he did especially for me. In the light of his oil lamp, he put a comb through a reproduction of Breughel's "Triumph of Death"; it was a revelation in how to sort out events in a picture.

Later he asked me if I would like to see a couple of nude drawings he had done of himself, adding that he did not like leaving them about with Mrs. Barnes around. I said that I would, he disappeared upstairs, and there were noises of furniture being moved, and of something heavy being slid down the stairs. Through the door he pushed the top of a trestle table, on which was pinned one of the drawings. They were over life-size and drawn on old wallpaper which he had got from Fairchild, the builder, as we had done years before from Mr. Bailey. When I asked him how he had managed them, he told me he had started with the head and went on pushing the paper over the end of the table top till the feet came up.

But these were not occasions when one could look closely at what he was painting. He would be around, making his comments; at times he could behave in an off-hand way in their presence. And sometimes I have felt that it is better to come on these pictures alone. They are very strange pictures—though not, one assumes, to the mind of a mystic, and in his own "chapel" way I think he was. They enabled me to better appreciate, throughout the changing situations of his life, his continual hammering of the spirit of "joy". This spirit is so much in the front of these pictures that to apply any other criteria would not be fitting. In these later works he tapped a new and totally unexpected source. Compare the woman smelling the sun-flower in "Sun-flower and Dog Worship" with Hilda smelling the flower in "The Resurrection"; their mystery deepens. All these pictures are "looking" eastward. The Beatitudes of Love in the way he painted them, are a profound expression of triumph. Almost at the same time he painted the Wilderness series. In most of these pictures his personality seems to be strongly present. He seems to have buried in them the mystery of his vision.

"The joy needed for creativeness can be and must be *subject to nothing*," he once wrote to me. "If in deed and fact one has got to take a hopeless and worldly view which the acceptance of insecurity would necessitate, *then* is Christ *not* crucified and our art of no avail, and then any General Dash's wife can come round the corner where one is painting and say, as she said to me in 1939, 'Ah, Mr. Spencer, you will have to put those brushes and palette away now'—in a gloating mood of, 'This war will stop all that nonsense anyway.' "

But the war did not, of course, stop "all that nonsense". For one thing, Stan then became one of the official "War Artists". For his series of pictures of shipbuilders at work, he lived for a time at Port Glasgow, staying with a footballer blacksmith and his wife. Joe Buchanan was a great athlete, who played for Celtic—"which produces a hush on any but ignoramuses such as ourselves", he wrote to me—and according to repute had the longest kick in Scotland, though when Stan mentioned this to him he replied, " 'Och, they're bumming mi hector'—which means Don't you believe it." On one occasion, when Stan mentioned that a registered envelope would be arriving with £10 in cash in it, "a great hush fell", and after a long pause Joe remarked, "Do ye no play cards?" Altogether he had a grand time at The Port, he said. He would walk home from the shipbuilders' up a glen in which the children picked blackberries, and had only to walk over the moors to be in Burns country.

Originally the Ministry of Information commissioned him to do one of these pictures, for £50, but he also worked out the big compositions, and when he showed these to them they were delighted and asked him to go ahead. He enjoyed doing them, and enjoyed working in the shipbuilding works, which he described as "dark and cosy and full of mysterious places and happenings, like a vast Cookham blacksmith's shop interior". While writing about them to me, he also expressed a mischievous desire—"one of the wishes of my life"—to do a design for a toilet roll; and he did in fact do a 35 feet long drawing on this scale, which he carried about rolled up in a box.

His strong feeling for place comes through again in "Villagers and Saints". Nelson Franks, the rag and bone merchant, never came to our front door to buy rags, bones and bottles, and the bullets which we used to collect from the butts on Cockmarsh Common when out for our walks with Annie; and it is the kitchen door that we see in the picture. But the bottles which he used to buy from us had passed out of circulation years before, and the bottles we see making a lovely pattern between him and the praying saint are those in which Vichy water is supplied—at the time Stan was having to drink it for his health. The milk jug and the milk book on the window-sill would have been a social slur on the drawing-room sill. I was a little puzzled for a moment as to what the scroll was resting on, and beneath which I am drawing the ring round the marbles. It had all the appearance of our kitchen door mat. Then I recalled that it was part of Alice's routine, when she was cleaning the kitchen, to fling out the mats without paying much attention to where they landed, and as often as not they landed on top of us—as they have done in the painting.

I have only attempted to describe these pictures in the way Stan and I talked about them when looking at them together. For the rest, what is so compelling about them remains for me hidden in a realm of sensation that is beyond language. When language itself gets too close to these experiences, it seems to make this other approach unrewarding, as though it sprang from a sourceless inspiration. He never gave me the impression of any slackening of his excitement about what he was doing.

I didn't know until he wrote of it that "St. Francis and the Birds", "Sarah Tubb and the Heavenly Visitors" and the other pictures of his period to which he refers were elements of which "Christ Preaching at Cookham Regatta" was also a part, though the method of putting the work together was different from the one he used for the Burghclere murals. Then he seemed to hold himself in check until he had got it all clear in his mind. Now he was troubled with detail. He was very insistent about perspective, and was worried about the figurehead of the *My Queen*. Somehow she did not seem right when seen from above, which displeased him. For a time she went out of the painting, to come back later in her present form—which is in perspective but not convincing. As children we had always seen her from below, towering up beneath the bowsprit. Now he removed the bowsprit altogether, and reconstructed rather than remembered her. I never saw any complete drawing for this picture. Sometimes he put drawings of parts of it together on the floor, to show me what it would be like, but I never had any visual impression of it as a whole in my mind, as one always had from his other big works through the drawings.

The conditions in which this work was being carried out were in a way a tragedy. If only somebody, or some institution, had come forward with a scheme to accommodate him and it properly some years before. Then much misfortune might have been avoided. His health was giving way; it is astonishing that he worked away at it as he did. How much it suffered in the circumstances can never be answered. I saw it pinned to the wall at Cliveden View, two-thirds rolled up, while he painted away at the rest. I saw it on the north wall behind the choir stalls in Cookham Church, with a concourse of people surging round. I again saw it pinned on the wall in his bedroom at the vicarage where he stayed with Mr. and Mrs. Westropp after his operation. Then he took his palette and brush and painted a little of the map, making the strange allusion that it was the colour of blood. And finally I saw it pinned to the wall of our bedroom at Fernley, saw him climb on to a table and then on to a chair on top of it, and again with the same little palette and brush paint a little of "Gouldens Backwater". Putting his head so close to the canvas that his nose almost touched it, he remarked as he did so, "If anyone wants to see my pictures, they want to get as near as this."

On one of my visits to Cliveden View, so small and restricted a place—he had only been put in there as a temporary arrangement by my brother Percy, but then discovered that in some peculiar way he had fallen in love with it—I was looking at a figure of a man. Without the picture in front of me I am not certain whether this figure was one that was retained or was finally discarded: he was holding a great turnip of a watch which he had taken from his trouser pocket, and was looking down the full length of his straightened arm to ascertain the time. Suddenly from behind me came the sharp voice of Stan, "'Arf 'arter six!", followed by his little look of recognition, as though to say "You remember him".

Now comes one of the most extraordinary comments I ever heard him make—and I leave it at that. I noticed that Christ and the Apostles were all wearing black boaters, and I remarked on this to him. Perhaps he regarded my enquiry as out of place or silly, though I don't think so. Anyway, he responded with "Chairman of the Watch Committee", and added one or two disapproving words regarding their power.

I noticed a terrifying pre-occupation with extraneous detail now. The artificial graining on the outside of the punts was never there: Mr. Bailey used to produce this "counterfeit" on our kitchen doors and dressers. And yet at this time he was writing to Mrs. Martineau, "Time is the important thing". I don't think there ever was a finer assembly of promise in any unfinished canvas, and I share the view that, had he been fit and the circumstances better, it might well have proved his finest achievement. As it stands it frightens me when I think of him alone in a room night and day painting it as he did. And one remembers that "The Crucifixion" had been housed in the same way and painted at the same time.

While he was painting this, Jill Henderson and I ran into him on Paddington Station. Our train was almost due to leave, and we squeezed into the window of the carriage to talk to him. He remembered that Miss Henderson had looked after him at Maidenhead Cottage Hospital and that he had drawn her, and in the remaining moments before the train left went straight on to this picture, about the design and what he called the area of the sky. And as we moved out he called after us, "And my God I've got something going on up there".

With all this work, the many demands for landscapes and portraits, his letter writing, and also an odd assortment of requests now that he was something in the nature of a public figure, he still found time to read, on one occasion reading a lot of "The Cotter's Saturday Night" to me, and, the last time I saw him at Fernley, whole reams of Belloc with tremendous verve.

His diary (a miniature Bible) was black with engagements. When my new bank manager paid me a visit and, in the course of our talk, remarked that though he had not had the pleasure of meeting me before, he knew my brother, he surprised me very much, as I knew that Stan had dispensed with banks altogether years before. To my further enquiry the manager told me that he had met him at the Maidenhead Chamber of Commerce.

At Cheltenham, where he was the guest speaker at an anti-litter campaign meeting, he devoted his speech very largely to declaring his love of and interest in litter.

"I made the best speech I have ever made at the Bank of England," he told me. And he made the worst at Camberwell School, where in two or three minutes he undid my cherished hopes by telling my students that he "never looked". It may have been popular but it was very inaccurate.

But with all these calls, and the distinctions that were now coming to him, there seemed to be no change in him. He wished he could wear his C.B.E. "all the time", and when his knighthood was announced, his "vanity" (his own word) took him up to Cookham Station and back to "see what people said". The last time Florence and I were with him at Fernley he gave us a performance of his investiture.

I sometimes wondered how much sleep he got, with so many calls, commissions and journeyings. He often was tired but not able to sleep. He had his afternoon rests, as he called them, sometimes just curling up on a chair with his feet tucked up beneath his greatcoat, which he would put on for these siestas.

He accepted an invitation to form one of a party to fly to Peking on a goodwill mission. It was a purely cultural occasion. After the decline of the Liberal Party, we searched for its attitude among the more moderate elements of the Socialist movement, but my brother's hatred of power made him reject all forms of extremism.

When he returned from China I telegraphed to him (he did not have a telephone). He rang me up, and what follows is his account of his visit:

Me: "Hullo, Stan. How did you get on?"
Stan (rather a tired voice): "All right."
Me: "What did it feel like?"
Stan: "Most of the Chinese are very modern and wear American jeans. I looked down some of the old streets but was too frightened to go down. I was so afraid, as I always am, of getting lost. As a matter of fact, I liked Siberia best."
Me (with memories of the Chinese crackers at home): "What about the Chinese crackers?" (There had been some kind of festival.)
Stan: "I didn't go. Some Mongolians or something came in, and I went upstairs."

When I asked him if he had done any painting, he said, 'Not a lot", and added that he had left what he had done on he aeroplane because he could not wait to get home. Afterwards he told me that he had "managed to do about a dozen drawings and finally two rather sketchy oil paintings of the Ming Tombs. I also began an oil painting of the

Summer Palace garden—just by a tree-bordered stream like one of the back streams at Cookham."

A few days later he came over and my wife, all agog, got out the atlas. He did point out some of the places he passed over, but he was mainly interested in telling us of the Russian method of sleeping in dormitories at the airports, how one of his companions on the flight snored, how he dragged his mattress into a lavatory and shut the door but still could not sleep, how he had returned and tried to turn the snorer off his back—"Good Lord, I thought I might push him out"—and how he then remembered how we turned patients in hospital. He went through the movements with his arms to remind me. But he had found the Siberian airports "rather cosy and Victorian". He showed us a little drawing in a notebook, the nose of his plane and in the distance Moscow.

He had "really rather enjoyed the flying". I asked him if he had been nervous and he said, "No, except when the engine went *fit! fit!! fit!!!* Then," he said, "I looked down into a forest and said to myself 'There are bears in there.' " He was very impressed by the size and colour of the Kremlin, and described the mechanism of the curtain at the Moscow theatre they visited, bringing his fist sharply into his other hand to emphasise the speed and impact. This, I felt, had a very Russian feeling for him.

He told us of the visit to Chou En-lai, and of his claim that the Chinese were a home-loving people, to which Stan had replied, "So am I. It took China to get me away from Cookham." But he stayed on after the others had returned and came home independently. He had been ill with a cold all through his stay. "The very kind Chinese were so worried and did all they could," he wrote to my wife, "the Chinese waiters conferring together and bringing me only what I could fancy, like toast and eggs and tea and suchlike." While he was there his weight dropped from around 8 stone 4 to 6 stone 10.

After this he settled down to his regatta picture and others for a while, and then came the exhibition in Cookham

Church organised by Michael Westropp to raise funds for the repairing of the church roof. This was to prove his final curtain. I watched him walking about among the thousands visiting it, with his daughters, and again his detachment was noticeable. He gave some talks, and the people were sitting three and four abreast down the aisles. From time to time he worked on a painting of the church, standing, unless I am mistaken, beneath the same elm tree by the kissing gate from which Father had shaken the little owl.

But the sands were running out. I did not hear any more of him until my brother Percy rang me up to tell me that he was in the Canadian Hospital at Cliveden. Together we went over, but we did not see him, and the report we got was so serious that we did not think we should ever see him again. But he recovered from this attack and was soon walking round the ward drawing heads, and occasionally sitting with other patients.

Ursula and I visited him and found him entirely self-possessed. He did not mention his illness, chivvied one of the nurses for going out when he wanted to go on with a drawing, and talked a lot about the mind. Cocked up behind him was a drawing-board on which was an unfinished drawing of a head. When I remarked on it he said, "I mean to have another go at it if I get half a chance." We came away astonished once more at his complete indifference to his physical situation.

He did have another chance, and he used it to the full. He went to friends in Yorkshire, where he painted his last self-portrait. He returned to village life and renewed his teas at the Copper Kettle and, against some protests, after his convalescence he moved into Fernley which had been bought for him by Lord Astor and Jack Martineau, instead of returning to his beloved Cliveden View. From there he went to Buckingham Palace to be knighted.

His return to Fernley had immediate public repercussions. I found myself twice featured with him, in John

London's column in the *News Chronicle* and later in Cliff Michelmore's T.V. programme "Tonight".

Being back at Fernley, after so much had happened, had an immensely nostalgic effect upon me. But it didn't seem to affect my brother: I don't think the passage of time moved him at all.

The last time I saw him out of hospital, Cash Martineau and I went over to Cookham and he came back to Old Lodge with us for supper. As usual when we were together, the conversation turned on Spencer lore; this time we gossipped about the very odd assortment of servants we had had. Then he returned to Cookham, to another party at Church Cottage. He wanted me to go with him and I wish I could have done, as very soon afterwards he was back in hospital. It was clear that he was not going to get better this time. I suggested to my daughter Gillian that she should go with me to the hospital, adding that we should probably not see him. As we walked down the passage, Gillian, who was in front of me, saw him through the partly opened door and turning to me whispered, "He's reading the *Observer*". And so he was, an account of Khrushchev's visit to the Pope. Although he was weak, there was not a sign of any diminution of his mental powers. He asked Gillian to read the article to him, after which he drew a circle in the air and pushed his index finger through the centre of it.

His room was smothered with those wonderful creations, "Get Well" cards, gloriously vulgar. He loved them, sent by many admiring young artists and students.

On a shelf was a flat cardboard box containing his hood, which had been conferred on him that year by Southampton University. He was very proud of this and wanted Gillian to put it on. How I prayed for a blueprint explaining how to put it on. I was afraid that our fumbling efforts might worry him, but they didn't. He beckoned Gillian over to his bed and, as she leaned over, he put it on her himself, and got it right.

We were joined by two of his friends, and in a whispered

conversation with them I referred to the unfinished "Resurrection". It was then that he wrote on a piece of paper his explanation that he had painted "Apple Gatherers" over it.

As a matter of interest, the left arm and hand of the man and the right arm of the woman in the foreground of that picture are his own.

The next evening my brother Percy rang me up to tell me that he had died peacefully.